MAN-EATERS OF MALEKULA

ROY BRANDSTATER

Pacific Press®
Publishing Association
Nampa, Idaho | Oshawa, Ontario, Canada
www.pacificpress.com

Cover design by Gerald Lee Monks
Cover design resources from Artkhade.com

Additional copies of this book can be obtained by calling toll-free 1-800-765-6955 or by visiting http://www.adventistbookcenter.com.

Library of Congress Cataloging-in-Publication Data
Names: Brandstater, Roy, author.
Title: Man eaters of Malekula / Roy Brandstater.
Description: Nampa, Idaho : Pacific Press Publishing Association, [2017]
Identifiers: LCCN 2017015634 | ISBN 9780816363049 (pbk. : alk. paper)
Subjects: LCSH: Seventh-day Adventists—Missions—Vanuatu—Malekula. | Missionaries—Vanuatu—Malekula. | Cannibalism—Vanuatu—Malekula. | Malekula (Vanuatu)—History.
Classification: LCC BV3676.A1 B73 2017 | DDC 266/.679595—dc23 LC record available at https://lccn.loc.gov/2017015634

March 2017

DEDICATION

This documented account is affectionately dedicated to the two intrepid couples—the only white missionaries to live among the Nambus man-eaters of Malekula—Norman and Alma Wiles, and Will and Louisa Smith, along with their two small sons, Ivan and Milton. Time may dim the impact of their years of service and sacrifice. But here we remember them.

Roy Brandstater
November 4, 1981

CONTENTS

Preface.......7
Introduction.......9
Chapter 1: Man-eaters of Malekula.......15
Chapter 2: John Williams, Martyr.......19
Chapter 3: Presbyterians Pave the Way.......23
Chapter 4: Adventists Join the Assault on Heathenism.......34
Chapter 5: Probing Mysterious Malekula.......39
Chapter 6: Norman and Alma Wiles.......44
Chapter 7: First Mission on Malekula.......48
Chapter 8: The Parkers Depart.......53
Chapter 9: Alma's Diary.......60
Chapter 10: Replacement for Norman Wiles.......76
Chapter 11: Heathen Hunger for a Better Way.......81
Chapter 12: Small Craft in Heavy Seas.......86
Chapter 13: Native Defiance.......91
Chapter 14: Many a Danger.......97
Chapter 15: The Fruit of Missions.......100
Chapter 16: A New Generation Takes Over.......104
Chapter 17: The Significant Sixties.......107
Chapter 18: Nambus Still Primitive—A 1965 Visit.......112
Chapter 19: Stepping Hopefully Into the Seventies.......119
Appendix I.......127
Appendix II.......129
Appendix III.......132
Appendix IV.......136
Bibliography.......138

PREFACE

"It is your duty to retell the vivid evidence of your terrible experience to your children and grandchildren, to your friends, colleagues, comrades. . . . Document it, write it. Tell it verbally. Don't let it be forgotten." With these words Yitzhak Navon, the president of Israel, challenged his people.

In much the same way, I felt compelled to research and document this account of Malekula. I had to do it or live under the frown of a task undone. The trials and hazards of Malekula in the raw must never be forgotten or denied.

Christian heroes and heroines in the South Pacific were consumed with the divine commission to "go into all the world and preach the gospel to every creature." They accepted the challenge and faced the dangers of serving a heathen and hostile people who lived and died by the only way they knew—without God and without hope.

Because of my personal acquaintance with some of those missionary pioneers, I feel compelled to put them on record—C. H. Parker, Harold Carr, A. G. Stewart, Norman and Alma Wiles, Will and Louisa Smith, and the Ross James and Don Nicholson families. These deserve more than casual comments hidden away in archives long forgotten. They ought to be remembered as honored examples of dedication, fortitude, and Christian courage.

These pioneers faced the dangers, suffered from fevers, battled with the elements, and even gave their lives. Their names ought to be engraved not only in bronze and marble but in the hearts of all Malekulans.

No efforts have been spared in documenting this record. I knew the missionaries personally, and I was graciously given access to back years of minutes at the Adventist headquarters office in Sydney, Australia. We also did research at the

Mitchell Library, Sydney; the Avondale Heritage Library, Australia; the Loma Linda Heritage Library, California; and other archives. In addition, we paged through sixty-nine years of the *Australasian Record,* a weekly journal that contained frequent reports of the doings of the missionaries in the New Hebrides from 1912 to 1981. (These reports have been condensed in places.)

I am deeply indebted to the late Alma Wiles, who shared with me her diary and her memories of mission adventures.

Looking back through all the dangers, dramas, tragedies, and triumphs, we can say that the results have been most rewarding and the sacrifices worthwhile in the rescue of hundreds who otherwise had no hope, as this account testifies.

The Author

INTRODUCTION

BY THE POPULAR RELIGIOUS COMMENTATOR

ROY ALLAN ANDERSON

Do you enjoy reading cannibal stories? Then this is the book for you, every word of which I know to be true. Not only do I know the author, but I have known many of the important personalities mentioned here.

A major part of this work has waited for more than fifty years to be documented. Now the true story of Malekula has been traced through the years and told in unblemished accuracy. This colorful record in all its drama and pathos gives the factual story of murderous cannibals who lived in a world of their own and resented an intrusion on their island domain. They were a law unto themselves and were unconscious of their need of another way of life.

When John G. Paton told his Green Street Church in Glasgow, Scotland, that he was going to the New Hebrides to preach the gospel of Christ, one of his church leaders remarked, "If you go to that hate-filled land, you will be eaten." He replied, "If I live and die knowing the Lord Jesus and sharing that knowledge with others, it will make no difference whether I am eaten by cannibals or eaten by worms." He went, and what an account of dangers, inhuman trial, and unmatched dedication is on his record! Some of these mission exploits are given in this book. It will be noted that at the age of thirty-two he and his young wife sailed for the New Hebrides, making their home on the island of Tanna. His wife died in childbirth the next year, and their baby son a week following, leaving him distraught and lonely to live and labor for thirty years on the edge of a proverbial hell.

To get the full impact of the story of *Man-eaters of Malekula*, it was necessary to recount the efforts of the first missionaries to land in the New Hebrides, such men as John Williams, James Gordon, and his brother, George Gordon, all of whom were brutally murdered on Erromango. Then there was H. A. Robertson, another Presbyterian missionary, who on learning of the second Gordon brother's murder, asked to be allowed to fill the martyr's place and continue his mission. He called upon the Scottish Christians to join in the prayerful slogan—"Erromango for Christ!" It took twenty-five years, but that prayer was answered. Who would have believed that this could happen to blood-soaked Erromango? This island became Christian. A church was built in memory of the martyrs, and Isaiah's words became a reality: "My people shall dwell in a peaceful habitation."

While some of these chapters will cause the reader to smile, others will be read with eyes brimming with tears. Yes, this is a moving story, following Norman and Alma Wiles, succeeded by Will and Louisa Smith. These were the only white missionaries to locate on Malekula, the first couple for five years, and the Smiths, with their two small boys, for more than seven years. Louisa Smith was the sister of Roy Brandstater, the author.

There are many near tragedies recorded in this book, but one of the most moving is the story of Norman and Alma Wiles. Their experience on Malekula began in 1914 and was no less loaded with hazards and problems of living among savages than Paton and other pioneers', C. H. Parker led the work in the New Hebrides, followed by A. G. Stewart. They were bold, dedicated, and courageous as they initiated the work on various islands. How they entranced us with their cannibal tales on returning to Australia! Parker was the first of the Seventh-day Adventists to New Hebrides.

Snippets of the Wileses' story have been told so many times that this missionary pair has become a legend in Australian mission history—how Alma in young womanhood suffered with her beloved Norman but could do little to save him from the dreaded blackwater fever. This lonely, traumatic experience is told in her diary, which was only discovered after Alma's death in March 1980. This book is the first to release this personal account.

Two years went by before Norman's place was filled by Will Smith, together with Louisa. Will came close to losing his life on several occasions, being tipped off a launch into the Pacific Ocean in the dead of night and later contracting the same frightening fever that took the life of his predecessor.

The last chapters of the book are a vivid portrayal of the progress of the missions in the New Hebrides and contrasting changes over the years. Many churches, schools (including a training school for indigenous workers), and

powerful Malekulan pastors have emerged from the haunts of heathenism and cannibalism. Even the political position has taken on a local administration, and government is no longer from France or Great Britain. Even the name of the island group was changed to Vanuatu in July 1980.

This book is more than a mission story; it is a documented account of miracles, drama, tragedy, and triumph.

NIKAMBAT, THE PARAMOUNT CHIEF

KING OF THE CANNIBALS

Nikambat, the king of the cannibals, known far and wide throughout the area, looked the part. Tall, well built, with long shaggy hair from which hung beads of small shells, he presented a rather awe-inspiring figure. He also had a long black beard, a polished round shaft of bone thrust through the centre of his nostrils, and was wearing bracelets of pig's tusks on his forearms. Around his waist were many rounds of plaited bark to which were attached the dark red bunch of twisted grass, or nambus, the only piece of covering as wearing apparel. With him were all of his warriors, similarly attired.

—Andrew G. Stewart on meeting Nikambat
"Among the Big Nambus in the New Hebrides,"
Review and Herald, June 25, 1959,
published in *The Australasian Record*, August 24, 1959

CHAPTER 1

MAN-EATERS OF MALEKULA

Of the eighty islands of the New Hebrides group, Malekula was the most primitive, the most heathen, and the most savage. Andrew G. Stewart, pioneer Adventist missionary to the South Pacific islands, wrote: "This is the saddest point in all the Pacific." John Geddie, Presbyterian missionary of the nineteenth century, wrote in his journal, "This is truly one of the dark places of earth, where all the abominations of the heathen are practiced without scruples and without remorse." My brother, Gordon Brandstater, who spent some twenty-five years supervising mission work in the Pacific, told me, "There is no place on earth where I have been that shows the degradation of mankind as I have seen on the island of Malekula."

Crimes of every kind were commonplace. The people considered theft and licentiousness honorable. There was apparently no human love, but in its place disaffection and malice. There was cruelty instead of sympathy; brutality instead of mercy; suspicion instead of trust; sullenness instead of smiles; warfare instead of peace; and fear instead of faith. No adult male went about unarmed; every man carried a club or a spear—or both—until the white trader came and provided muskets.

Pigs were the main article of barter until recent years. A wife cost an average of ten pigs. The animals shared human living quarters and were treated as prime property. In March 1980, Pastor Sam Dick, a native of Malekula, visited me in my home in Redlands, California. I asked him about his parents. In reply he said, "Oh, my father killed my mother."

"Why would he do such a terrible thing?" I asked.

As if it were not an unusual thing to do, he answered straightway, "Oh, he had a very special pig, which had to do with our tribal worship. It was kept in the house; mother was its keeper, and it must not be let out. Somehow it found its way to freedom, and father saw it outside wallowing in the mud. He was so angry he took his club and killed my mother. Then he took me as a baby to a widow to care for me. She said, 'No! You killed your wife; now you take care of your own baby.' So he killed her also. Then he gave me to my mother's sister, who was just a girl at the time, warning, 'Take care of this baby or I will kill you too!' "

THE EXPLORERS

Malekula is the second-largest island of the New Hebrides group, whose eighty islands reach out over the Pacific Ocean two thousand miles from Australia like two arms forming the letter Y. The islands were discovered by Pedro Fernandes de Queirós, a Spanish explorer. In 1605 he was searching for the "Great South Land," under instructions from the king of Spain, when he stumbled on one of the larger islands of the group.

When it became generally known that the earth was not flat but a sphere hanging in space, explorers and philosophers argued that there had to be a great land mass down under to keep the balance. This must be hidden away south of the equator, which was thought to be a blazing, impassable furnace.

In the fifteenth century Spain and Portugal were the world superpowers, competing for trade, treasure, and colonies. The pope, anxious to contain dangerous rivalries, divided the world between the two. They could now go their way and discover new lands and people, but they were committed to carry their religion to every race of people they might find.

Queirós, a deeply religious man, acclaimed this strange new outpost to be the "Great South Land of the Holy Spirit"—"*Australia del Espiritu Santo.*" When his men mutinied and provisions were almost exhausted, Queirós spent only fifteen days in this area, then sailed northwest through the straits separating Australia from New Guinea. Torres, his navigator, was left behind on another ship. Torres sailed through those same straits, giving them more attention, so that they were permanently named "Torres Straits." Likewise the island of Santo, New Hebrides, still retains the name Queirós gave it.

For 168 years after Queirós, these islands remained in isolation. Then in 1774 came the colorful Captain James Cook of Britain, searching for the "Great Southern Continent." His instructions were: "If you discover nothing westward to Tasman's New Zealand, you are to observe with accuracy the situation

of such islands as you may discover in your voyage that may not have been discovered by Europeans, and take possession for His Majesty; and endeavor by all proper means to cultivate friendship with the natives." Captain Cook rediscovered the New Hebrides and identified Santo and the Bay of St. Philip and St. James, named by Queirós. Then he charted this island along with other islands of the group, putting them accurately on the map, and named them after the Hebrides off the coast of Scotland.

The explorer wrote, "The people . . . are of a dark color, a little slender they have thick lips and flat noses; and monkey faces, long heads and wooly hair. What adds to their deformity is a cord, or belt around the waist, just under the short rib and over the middle of the belly, that is tied so tight they look as if they had two bellies." Captain Cook apparently did not venture far inland, nor did he elaborate on their habits. That remained for later visitors to describe.

ENTER THE MISSIONARIES

"You will be eaten by cannibals!" an elderly parishioner warned John G. Paton when, at the age of thirty-two, he decided to leave his congregation at Green Street, Glasgow, for the hate-filled heathen of the New Hebrides, a people little different from the wild beasts in their treatment of visitors.

"If I can live and die honoring the Lord Jesus," Paton replied, "it will make no difference whether I am eaten by cannibals or eaten by worms." Four months after leaving Scotland, when he landed on Tanna, he wrote, "I must confess, my first impressions drove me to the verge of utter dismay. On beholding these natives in their paint and nakedness and misery, my heart was as full of horror as of pity. Had I given up my work in Glasgow, with so many delightful associations, to consecrate my life to these degraded creatures? Was it possible to teach them right and wrong? Could we Christianize or even civilize them?" But he added, "That was only a passing feeling."

Cannibalism was a way of life, along with vicious, inhuman warfare. After the fight, victors ate the vanquished. John Paton and his wife had hardly arrived on Tanna when they were treated to a display of tribal warfare. "The discharge of muskets and the horrid yells of the savages informed us that they were engaged in deadly fights," he wrote.

> Excitement and terror was high. Armed men rushed around in every direction, with feathers in their twisted hair. Faces were painted red, black, white, some had one side painted black and the other red, others the brow white, the chin blue, in fact any color on any part—the more grotesque

> the higher the art. The women and children rushed to safety. We hid in a native house. We were told that six men had been killed and their bodies were cooked and eaten that night at a boiling spring. The next morning we were unable to use the water, it being polluted with the bodies and blood.

Paton said their mission boy was more upset about being unable to obtain pure water than about the cannibal feast, which he took for granted.

Trading ships were sometimes captured and the crews killed and eaten. A Sydney whaler, the *Royal Sovereign*, was wrecked on the island of Efate. The natives pretended to be helpful but suddenly attacked the crews. Only one man, John Jones, managed to escape with the help of a Samoan mission teacher, Mose. One missionary said that he saw a native slice flesh from a victim and eat it raw.

In 1853 a London Missionary Society ship left two Polynesian teachers with their wives and one little boy on the west coast of the island of Lelepa. John Feddis, who was there at the time, wrote of the warm reception given the teachers. But the natives were treacherous—nineteen days later the four mission workers were killed and eaten. The boy was spared, as the people thought to keep him. However, he kept crying, so they tied a stone around his neck and dropped him into the sea.

Christianized teachers from other islands were no less consecrated to their task. Two Samoan teachers, Apela and Samuela, were placed on the island of Futuna, where the chief promised to protect them. They were still there twelve months later when the mission ship returned, so the mission boat left Samuela's wife and daughter off on the island. When sickness broke out on the island, the natives blamed the mission teacher. The natives killed Apela, Samuela, and his daughter in their garden and then rushed to the house, where Samuela's wife was alone. The native leader, Nasaua, offered to spare her life if she would become his wife. This she refused to do, so he struck her down with a club. They took the teacher's goods, burned his house, and decked themselves with the family's clothing for heathen dances. Variations of this tragedy were repeated throughout the history of missions in the New Hebrides. One must wonder at the fortitude and dedication of those servants of God, brown and white, who risked everything to take the light of the gospel to those who sat in darkness.

CHAPTER 2

JOHN WILLIAMS, MARTYR

No account of mission work in the New Hebrides would be complete without mention of John Williams, the first martyr in the New Hebrides. He was "God's key man in the evangelizaton of the Southwest Pacific." When he was twenty-one years of age, he joined the London Missionary Society, married Mary Chauncer, a young woman of eighteen, and in 1818 was sent with his bride to Raiatea in the Society Islands. At the age of twenty-three, he was brimming over with talent and enthusiasm—and useful characteristics that included business acumen, the ability to learn languages easily, dedication, faith, and leadership—all of which gave him a great capacity for service.

Under the power of God, Williams conquered cannibalism on Raiatea, Rargonga, and other islands. Heathen gods were thrown into the flames, and many established a new way of life. Now he looked across the ocean for more heathen strongholds to conquer. Many more islands were out there, some with deeper depravity than the islands just Christianized. But the nearest lay a thousand miles away.

"O for a ship! A ship! A ship!" he confided to Mary. But he would need a ship of seventy or eighty tons to sail this trackless ocean. Mary knew what it would mean to her and to John and the work to which he was committed, so she finally consented. John decided to build himself a ship, a seemingly impossible task. There were no facilities, no equipment, and there was no iron except a cable chain left behind by a ship's crew fleeing for their lives. There was no forge, so he made a bellows from goatskins and an anvil from a big stone. Then he made his own

nails from the chain and the ironwood tree. He made ropes from the bark of the hibiscus tree, and for sails he used large woven native mats that he reinforced so they could withstand the wind. The ship was sixty feet long, weighed an estimated seventy or eighty tons, and was named *The Messenger of Peace.*

Now Williams was free, and the southwest Pacific was his parish—cannibals and all. What a world of evangelism opened before him! He made voyages to the Society Islands, Tonga, Samoa, the Cook Islands, and finally to the New Hebrides. His first step was the notorious island of Erromango, where Captain James Cook escaped under a shower of spears and arrows. In 1839, Williams sold *The Messenger of Peace*—the boat had outlived its usefulness. He had recently visited Scotland, where he recounted his mission adventures throughout the country and raised the money for another ship, larger and more suitable to the needs of the southern seas.

THE FIRST MARTYRS

The new mission ship, the brig *Camden*, was bought with contributions from people all over the British Isles. John Williams sailed in her from London with sixteen other missionaries. In November 1839, Williams set out with twelve Polynesian teachers aboard to open up work in the New Hebrides. He well knew the dangers, for these islands were famed for savagery. At his home island, many people came to bid him farewell. His wife's last words to him were, "Don't land on Erromango!"

A young man from England named Harris, who was on the voyage for his health, decided to join the mission program. Also Britain's vice-consul for the Pacific, a Mr. Cunningham, went ashore on Erromango with Williams in a boat. Captain Morgan and four crewmen took them to the stony beach at Dillon's Bay. The absence of women with the people standing on shore was a sinister sign, as Captain Morgan later remarked. As the natives went back into the bush, the three men followed. Suddenly the Erromangoans turned and rushed them, striking Harris and Williams down with clubs at the water's edge. Cunningham saved himself by throwing a stone into the face of a killer. It was impossible to retrieve the bodies, and when a man-of-war came later and caught up with the murderers, they said, "We ate them." The bones and skulls were taken to Samoa for burial, and a great wail went up from a hundred islands.

The martyrdom of John Williams at the age of forty-three darkened the night of the New Hebrides, but it reinforced the need for someone to bring a light. Rather than intimidate, the tragedy gave an impetus to further mission effort. Other young men with their wives came to fill the gaps of the

fallen. Rev. Dr. John I. Geddie, Rev. George N. Gordon, John G. Paton, Rev. S. F. Johnston, with their wives, came in 1857 under the sponsorship of the Presbyterian Church. These were champions of the cross of Christ—dedicated, capable, with a deep sense of sacred duty. "They loved not their lives unto death." Four of them never returned to their homeland. Mrs. Paton died on Tanna in childbirth, also suffering from malaria. Reverend Johnston, though young and vigorous, succumbed to an epidemic of measles that devastated several islands in 1861. On Erromango, where the Reverend Gordon and his wife were located, the natives blamed the missionaries for a hurricane that struck the island and murdered them with axes. "A great wave of missionary zeal passed over the home church as the tragic news of the Gordons was received. The members recognized more than ever the greatness of their task. Three missionaries immediately responded to an appeal for service in the New Hebrides."

Among those who volunteered was James D. Gordon, brother of the martyred George Gordon. He went right back into the area of those who murdered his brother, not for revenge but to redeem the murderers.

Coming from Prince Edward Island, he stepped right into his brother's place on Erromango in 1864. Eight years later he too was murdered. At the time, he was translating the Bible into the native language—ending in Acts 7, where Stephen was stoned and cried out, "Lord Jesus, receive my spirit and lay not this sin to their charge!"

The Reverend H. A. Robertson had just returned with his wife from Prince Edward Island to mission headquarters at Aneityum, and this was the first news that greeted him. He slipped a note into the hand of the mission director, stating that he would like to take Gordon's place. These men had prayed for "Erromango for Christ," and after twenty-five years, five martyrdoms, many dangers, patient labors, and personal sacrifices, their prayer was answered. Christ had conquered. A church was built at Dillon's Bay in memory of the martyrs. No cannibals remained, only Christians; no wars, only peace; no savages, only softened characters; no fears, for "My people shall dwell in a peaceable habitation . . . and quiet resting places."

SANDALWOOD AND SOUR NATIVES

Early traders who might have prepared the way for civilization were often little better than the natives themselves, except that the Europeans were not cannibals. These traders broke every rule of good human behavior, and they created an attitude of hostility toward the white man, especially toward the missionary.

Many stole wood, took the women, and kidnapped the men to work on other islands, never to return. All the early mission writers complained of this as the chief reason for natives' hostility toward the whites.

The natives wanted the white man's knives, axes, and muskets. They also wanted liquor and tobacco. The sandalwood traders were some of the first and most notorious to exploit the natives and make them "more a child of hell" than they already were. John G. Paton found these traders exasperating in their opposition to the mission, countering all the good he was trying to do. He wrote in his autobiography,

> The sandalwood traders are as a class the most godless of men, whose cruelty and wickedness make us ashamed to own them as our countrymen. By them the poor, defenseless natives are oppressed and robbed on every hand; and if they offer the slightest resistance, they are ruthlessly silenced by the musket or revolver. Few months here pass without some of them being shot, and instead of their murderers being ashamed, they boast of how they dispatched them. Indeed all traders here are able to maintain their position only by revolvers and rifles. . . . A common cry was: "Let them perish, and let the white man occupy these islands." It was such conduct as this that made the islanders suspect all foreigners and hate the white man and seek revenge in robbery and murder.

After the sandalwood came the recruiting of labor, another blot on the pages of Pacific Island history. This included the scandalous Kanaka trade, the kidnapping of natives to work for sandalwooders on other islands, or in Queensland, where cotton and sugarcane were the main crops needing manual labor. Seventy men were recruited by Benjamin Boyd for his sheep ranch in New South Wales, all from Tanna, Lifu, and Uvea of the Hebrides. They eventually escaped, some finding their way back to their island homes, but most lost in the battle to survive.

Finally the Pacific Islands Laborers Act was enforced in 1901, which eliminated the trade of native islanders and sent the traders back home.

CHAPTER 3

PRESBYTERIANS PAVE THE WAY

Among the pioneers of the gospel, for high adventure, hairbreadth escapes, and miracles in mission lands, John G. Paton stands out as a prime example of fortitude, faith, and devotion to duty. He spent thirty years among New Hebrides cannibals and had seemingly reached the limits of life more often than it is possible to survive without a miracle. For most of us, one hairbreadth escape in a lifetime is enough; but with this Christian giant, perils such as hurricanes, plagues, and wars, which took the lives of hundreds around him, were taken for granted. Many times he stared down the barrel of a musket or warded off a club or fantail tomahawk that was raised to smash his skull; other times it was a knife poised over his heart or a quivering spear in the hands of a killer.

John G. Paton and his young wife landed on Tanna on November 5, 1858. Less than a year later she died in childbirth, and their little son died a week later. Paton, thirty-four, was stunned by his terrible loss. He wrote, "Let those who have ever passed through any similar darkness as of midnight feel for me as for all others. It would be more than vain to try to paint my sorrow." The missionaries assembled at Tanna on April 27, 1859, felt the loss almost as keenly as he, and they urged him to return to the Aneityum mission headquarters for a break. But he declined, saying, "If I leave, the natives would not let me return to this island. I am determined to hold as long as possible, though feeling very weak, and suffering badly from the aque [perhaps malaria]."

Tanna had a record of resentment and hate toward missions, though the Reverend W. J. Matheson and his wife were invited to locate there and promised

protection by a chieftain. Like Malekula, it was one of the most dangerous islands of the group. Before the arrival of Paton and Matheson, the London Missionary Society had placed the Reverends Dr. George Turner and Henry Nisbet there, in 1842. But seven months later they barely escaped with their lives. Tanna was nearest to Erromango, and the Tannese hailed the murder of Williams and Harris with rejoicing. Paton tells of a case when not only were slain men eaten, but their widows were strangled and added to the gruesome orgy.

CHALLENGING DEVILRY

The New Hebrides do not lack gods, despite their degraded customs. In fact, there is an abundance of gods. They have stone idols, charms, and sacred objects of which they live in perpetual fear. "The Tannese," wrote Paton, "are ceaselessly groping after God. They make idols and gods of almost everything—trees and groves, rocks and stones, springs and streams, insects and animals, men and spirits, heavenly bodies and volcanoes. And they worship their chiefs, who wield great power over them."

Paton wrote in his autobiography,

> One day I held a service, in the village where morning after morning their tribes assembled, and declared that if they would believe and follow the Jehovah God, He would deliver them from all their enemies and lead them into a happy life. There were present three sacred men, of whom the whole population lived in terror—professors of sorcery, claiming the powers of life and death, health and sickness, rain and drought, according to their will. On hearing me, these three stood up and declared that they did not believe in Jehovah, nor did they need His help, for they had the power to kill [me] by *Nahak* [sorcery or witchcraft], if only they could get possession of any piece of fruit or food of which I had eaten. This was an essential condition of their black art; hence the peel of a banana, or an orange, or a broken scrap of food was gathered up by the natives, lest it should fall into the hands of sacred men and be used for *Nahak*. This superstition was the cause of most of the bloodshed and terror on Tanna. Being thus challenged, I asked God's help and determined to strike a blow against it.
>
> A woman was standing by with a bunch of native fruit in her hand, like plums, called *quoquore*. I asked her to give me some, and she, holding out a bunch, said, "Take freely what you will!" Calling the attention of all the assembly to what I was doing, I selected three fruits out of the bunch and took a bite from each. I gave them one after another to the three sacred

men and deliberately said in the hearing of all, "You have seen me eat of this fruit, you have seen me give the remainder to your sacred men, who have said that they can kill me by *Nahak*. I challenge them to do it if they can, without arrow or spear, club or musket; for I deny that they have any power against me, or against anyone by their sorcery!"

The challenge was accepted; the natives looked terror-struck at the position in which I had placed myself! The ceremony of *Nahak* was usually performed in secret—the Tannese eagerly watched their ritual. As the three chiefs arose and drew near one of the sacred trees to begin their ceremony, the natives fled in terror, crying, "Missi, Tawe! Alas, Missi!" But I held on at my post of observation. Amid wavings and incantations, they rolled the pieces of the fruit from which I had eaten in certain leaves of the sacred tree, into a shape like a wax candle. Then they kindled a sacred fire near the root and continued their mutterings, gradually burning a little more and a little more of the candle-shaped things, wheeling them round their heads, blowing upon them with their breath, waving them in the air, and glancing wildly at me as if expecting my sudden destruction. Wondering after all whether they did not believe their own lie, for they seemed to be so dead in earnest, I, more eager than ever to break the chains of such superstition, urged them again and again, crying, "Be quick! Stir up your gods to help you! I am not killed yet; I am perfectly well!"

Every day throughout that week the conch shells were sounded, and on that side of the island all their sacred men were at work trying to kill me by their arts. Now and again messengers arrived from every quarter of the island inquiring anxiously after my health, and wondering if I was not feeling sick. Great excitement prevailed. Sabbath dawned upon me peacefully, and I went to that village in more than my usual health and strength. Large numbers assembled and when I appeared, they looked at each other in terror, as if it could not really be myself still spared and well. Entering into the public ground, I saluted them to this effect; "My love to you all, my friends: I have come again to talk to you about the Jehovah God and His worship."

The three men admitted that they had tried to kill me by *Nahak*, but had failed. On being asked why they failed, they gave the subtle reply that I also was a sacred man and that my God was stronger than theirs, and had protected me from their gods. In addressing the multitude I answered, "Yes, truly my Jehovah God is stronger than your gods. He protected me and helped me; for He is the only living and true God, the only God who can hear and answer you, if you will give your hearts and lives to Him, and

> love and serve Him. This is my God, and He is your friend if you will hear and follow His voice."

Paton tells how he then sat down with the people around him, two of the sacred men also listened; but the third, a tall man of high rank, went off to get his spear. He returned brandishing it in the air and pointing it at Paton. "I said to the people, 'Of course he can kill me with his spear, but he undertook to kill me by *Nahak*, and promised not to use any weapon of war against me. If you let him kill me now, you will kill your friend, one who lives among you and only tries to do you good, as you all know well.' " The people then packed closely around Paton so that the killer dared not throw his spear.

For weeks after this, that sacred man followed the missionary about with his spear. Paton tells how he would suddenly appear on the path behind him, the spear posed in his right hand to strike. "God only kept it from being thrown," said Paton.

A SACRIFICIAL FEAST

"Missi, six or seven men have been shot dead for a great feast. It is to reconcile tribes that have been at war, and to allow a banished tribe to return in peace." One of Paton's teachers brought this word to Paton one morning. Before daylight the sacred men had allocated a murderer to the door of each house where an intended victim slept. A signal shot was fired; all rushed to their doors, and the doomed ones were shot or clubbed to death as they attempted to escape, Paton records. Their bodies were then borne to a sacred tree and hung up by the hands for a time as an offering to their gods. "Information had reached me," he wrote,

> that my teachers and I were destined victims for the same feast; and sure enough we saw a band of armed men, the killers dispatched toward our premises. Instantaneously I had the teachers and their wives and myself securely locked into the mission house. Cut off from all human hope, we set ourselves to pray. All through that morning and forenoon we heard them tramping around our house, whispering to each other, and hovering near our window and door. . . . All through that dreadful morning and far into the afternoon we thus stayed together.
>
> Toward sundown, constrained by the Invisible One, they withdrew from our mission house and left us in peace once more. . . . For many days we had to take unusual care and not expose ourselves to danger.

Paton tells how the cannibals bore away the slain to be cooked, distributed among the tribes, and eaten in their feast of reconciliation. It was a covenant sealed in blood but soon disregarded in another bloody war.

HEATHENISM'S HATE AND HORRORS

The heathen declared that they hated the Christians' worship because it made the natives afraid to continue their wars, their murders, their strangling of wives, and the eating of human flesh. The missionary was a living rebuke. John Paton, though urged many times to abandon the island and leave them to their heathenism, was constrained to remain at his post with the hope of saving them for Christ and transforming them into civilized Christians. "The heathen seldom slackened their hateful designs against my life," he wrote in his journal.

> When a large number of people were assembled at my house, a man furiously rushed at me with an axe. But a chief snatched a spade with which I had been working and dexterously defended me from instant death. Life in such circumstances led me to cling very near to the Lord Jesus. I knew not for one brief hour when or how an attack might be made. Trials and hairbreadth escapes strengthened my faith, and seemed only to nerve me for more to follow.
>
> One day, while toiling away at my house, the war chief, and his brother, and a large party of armed men surrounded the plot where I was working. They all had muskets, besides their own native weapons. They watched me some time in silence, then every man leveled a musket straight at my head. Escape was impossible. Speech would only have increased my danger. My eyesight came and went for a few moments. I prayed to my Lord Jesus, asking Him to protect me. . . . I tried to keep working on at my task as if no one was near me. In that moment, as never before, the words came to me, "If ye shall ask anything in my name I will do it," and I knew I was safe. Retiring a little from their first position, no words having been spoken, they took up the same certain attitude somewhat farther off, and seemed to be urging one another to fire the first shot. But restrained once again, they withdrew, leaving me with a new reason for trusting God.

ESCAPE FROM TANNA

Paton's escape from Tanna and the wreckage of the mission reads like fiction in John Paton's journal and autobiography. There were so many moments when instant

death seemed certain that one must conclude that Paton, like Job, lived under the divine restraining order, "Only do not lay a hand on his person" (Job 1:12, NKJV).

In January 1862, war raged on his side of the island between inland and coastal tribes. This one was worse than usual, involving many tribes. "We were in the midst of it," recorded Paton.

> Muskets were blazing all around our house. Miaki [the leading war chief of the island] had fled, and his followers took shelter around our house. He sent messages to other tribes, also presents, to come and fight against Missi and the Tannese who were friends of the worship. "Let us cook his body and Abraham's [the native Christian teacher], and distribute them to every village this side of the island!" Yet Miaki assured me that he had sent a friendly message. The inland people now fired into my house and beat against the walls with their clubs. They smashed in the door and windows of our storeroom, broke open boxes and casks, tore my books to pieces, scattered them about and carried off everything, including my boat and sails. . . . They plundered Abraham's house, and then made a rush at the bedroom where we were locked, firing muskets, yelling and trying to break in. A chief professing to be sorry for us called me to the window, but on seeing me sent a tomahawk through it, crying, "Come on, let us kill him now!" I replied, "My Jehovah God will punish you; a man-of-war will come and punish you if you kill Abraham, his wife, or me." He retorted, "It's all lies about a man-of-war! They did not punish the Erromangoeans. They are afraid of us. Come on, let us kill them!"
>
> He raised his tomahawk and aimed to strike my head. Many muskets were uplifted to shoot, so I raised a revolver and pointed it at them. The Reverend Joseph Copeland had left it with me on a previous visit. I did not wish it, but he insisted that the very knowledge that I had it might save my life. This time it did so, though it was harmless. The assailant dropped to the ground crying, "Missi has got a short musket! He will shoot you all!" After lying on the ground for a while they ran to the nearest bush. Towards nightfall they left us, loaded with plunder. So God once more graciously protected us.

Paton could see that this was no passing incident. Miaki and other chiefs intended to eliminate the mission.

> We learned that he had hired a group of killers to murder us the next morning. After talking with Miaki I left with a heavy heart, he was bent

on our destruction. In the darkness of the morning hours we dare not light a candle to give our position away. But when daylight came Miaki himself stood and blew a great conch shell, I ran out to see why this call to arms, and found it was the signal for a great company of howling armed savages to rush down the hill from the other side of the bay and made straight for the mission house. We had not a moment to lose. To have remained would have been certain death to us all, and also for Matthew, a teacher just arrived from Mr. Matheson's station, the other side of the island. Escape for life was now the only path of duty. There was not a moment left to take anything with us. We lost all our earthly goods excepting the clothes we had on. My Bible, the few translations which I had made into Tannese, and a light pair of blankets I carried with me.

To me the loss was bitter. All my deceased wife's costly outfits, her piano, silver, cutlery, books, etc., with which her dear parents had provided her, besides all that I had in the world. . . . The Sandalwood traders bought all the stolen property for tobacco, powder, balls and caps and shot. We could not take the path along the beach, for there our enemies would have quickly overtaken us. We entered the bush with the hope of getting away unobserved. But a cousin of Miaki, evidently secreted to watch us, sprang from behind a breadfruit tree, swinging his tomahawk, aimed it at my brow with fiendish look. Avoiding it, I turned upon him and said in a firm voice, "If you dare to strike me, my Jehovah God will punish you. He is here to defend me now!" With my eye fixed on him I gradually moved backward into the track, and God mercifully restrained him from following.

We reached Nowar's village and found the people terror-stricken, crying, and rushing about in despair at seeing such a host of savages approaching. They threw away their weapons and cast themselves headlong on the ground, knocking their heads against the trees as if courting death before it came. They cried, "Missi, it is no use. We will all be killed and eaten today!" Nowar was a friendly chief who had defended us as best he could. He had been wounded with a spear in his knee. As he saw the multitude approaching he said, "Missi, sit down beside me and pray to our Jehovah God, for if He does not send help now we are all dead men. They will kill us all on your account, and that quickly. Pray and I will watch."

We prayed as only one can pray when in the jaws of death, and on the brink of eternity. We felt that God was near, and Omnipotent to do what seemed best. When the savages were about three hundred yards off, at the foot of the hill leading up to the village, Nowar touched my knee saying, "Missi, Jehovah is hearing! They are all standing still."

Had they come on they would have met no opposition, for Nowar's men were all scattered in terror. On gazing shorewards, and around the harbor, as far as we could see was a dense host of warriors, but all were standing still, and apparently absolute silence prevailed. We saw a messenger running along the approached multitude, delivering some tidings and then disappearing into the bush. To our amazement, the host began to turn and slowly marched back in silence, and entered the remote bush at the head of the harbor. Nowar and his people were in ecstasy, crying out "Jehovah has heard Missi's prayer! Jehovah has protected us and turned them back!" I know not why they turned back; but I have no doubt that it was the doings of God to save our lives.

After some wrangling palaver, the whole mass attacked another village where they murdered two men, two women, and two children. The inhabitants fled, but all the enfeebled and children who fell into their hands were killed and eaten. Led on by Miaki, they then plundered and burned seven villages. At night time Miaki sent messages to Nowar, threatening to kill him and his people for protecting me, and there was great excitement. So it was decided that I should leave the village before morning. He advised me to try to get to Matheson's station, the other side of the island. But he refused to let me take any of my property. The danger was so great that Nowar said, "You cannot remain here any longer. My son will guide you to the large chestnut tree in my plantation. Climb up into it and remain there till the moon rises." Being at the mercy of doubtful friends, I, though perplexed, thought it best to obey. I climbed the tree, and was left there alone in the bush. Through the darkness, the hours I spent there still live in my memory. I heard the discharge of musket and the yells of the savages, yet I felt safe in the branches as if in the arms of Jesus.

About midnight Nowar sent his son to call me down, and to guide me to the shore where he was waiting for me. He said I was to go by canoe, and all was made ready, but altercations and treachery over this prevented me from going by the canoe we had hired. At night we set out in a frail canoe but were [driven] back by heavy seas.

PREPARING FOR THE LAST AND THE WORST

As I sat meditating on the beach after the night attempt by canoe, Faimungo, a friendly Inland chief, Nowar's son-in-law, warned us that the danger

was very great. All Nowar's men had fled, and Miaki was holding a meeting not a half-mile away, preparing to fall upon us. "Farewell Missi," he said, "I am going home. I don't want to see the work and the murders of this morning." I asked if he would let us follow him, or show us the path. "When the Mission ship arrives I will give you three good axes, blankets, knives and many things you prize." He said, "Missi, you will be killed. I dare not let you follow. I have only about twenty men, and your following will endanger us all." I urged him to leave at once and we will follow at our own accord. I would not ask him to protect us; but if he betrayed us I assured him our God would punish him. If he spared us he would be well rewarded. He had with him seven men, thirteen were with Miaki. He would not call them. He said, "I will go; but if you follow me you will be killed on the way. You may follow me as far as you can."

About four miles on our way we met a party of Miaki's men. Some were for shooting us, and every musket was leveled at us; but Faimungo poised his spear and said, "No, you shall not kill Missi today!" A second hostile party encountered us, and with great difficulty we got away from them. Then another party intercepted us and were eager for our lives; but Faimungo encircled us, and said, "I am not afraid now, I am near my own land." Hurrying on, he sat down in a village dancing ground and said, "We can rest now." But in a few minutes he and his men started up. Down the mountain behind the village came the shouting and the rush of men toward us. Faimungo planted his back against a tree, and the others stood near me. They were the most powerful men that I had seen on the island, all flushed with their success at war. They encircled us in a deadly ring. They kept urging one another to kill us, but I said, "If you kill us my Jehovah God will punish you now and hereafter." My heart rose up to the Lord Jesus for protection; and it was as if I saw Him watching the scene. My peace came back to me like a wave from God. I felt immortal till my work was done. Yet I cannot say that I was without fear. Faimungo urged that we should go on. I said, "Why are we to leave you? My God heard your voice not to betray me. I will not leave you, and if I am to die, I will die by your side." He said, "Now I go on before, Missi; keep close to me." I followed with the teachers, praying the Lord to protect us; for the host of armed men ran alongside of us each with his weapons ready. I ran on in trust, as if they were my escorts, or as if I saw them not.

There was no explanation for the restraining of these killers, except for the same Divine hand that closed the lions' mouths for Daniel. The party had to

cross a stream, which they all did with an extra leap. All made it but Paton, the last to catch up with the group. He struck the bank and slid back to the water. Just then a native crashed a killing stone into a branch near where his head would have been. "At every village," he said, "enemies of the mission were ready to shoot us, but I kept close to Faimungo, knowing that he was the most influential chief in this area." However, at the end of his territory he bade Paton farewell and left the party to make their way through the final peril of the journey without a guide. The danger and excitement of the race for life kept them from collapse, though they were weak from exertion and lack of food.

The Mathesons were also in deep trouble. Together the missionaries prayed for support and guidance, for the mission here was also threatened. Every day of survival was a miracle. Early one morning, just as the mission's enemies had appointed that day to kill them all and plunder the mission, there was a cry, "Sail O! Sail O!" The ship had been sent from Aneitym to rescue the missionaries if alive. There was nothing else to do but leave, for to remain would have been "to incur the guilt of self-murder," Paton recorded. They had lost everything, and "now God had in answer to prayer, provided a way of escape."

The conquest of the Cross in the New Hebrides is the continuing story of the battle of the ages, the fight between good and evil, light and darkness. The heathen may appear to win, but the conflict has never ceased since Cain killed his brother Abel. Truth triumphs ultimately as light dispels darkness.

Paton's and Matheson's departure from Tanna was not the end of mission efforts on this island of tragedy. Nor was it the first setback; it was the fifth, in fact. Tanna wallowed in wars, murders, and cannibalism. In 1840 two Samoan teachers died; 1842 saw the Reverends Henry Nisbet and George Turner barely escape in a small boat. In 1845 the teacher Vasa was attacked and murdered. In 1847 teacher Pita escaped in a borrowed boat. In the years 1858 to 1860, the Mathesons lost their child and Paton lost his wife; Reverend Johnston died and the others barely escaped, leaving the island without a teacher or white missionary.

John Paton was despondent on leaving Tanna to its heathen fate. Besides, there had been some response—a number of friendly tribes could be called semi-Christian, and true followers left behind were in grave danger now. From the mission headquarters at Aneitym, Paton would gladly have returned if conditions allowed. However, those administering the work at the mission base, Reverend Geddie and Reverend Copeland, urged him to go to Australia in the interests of the mission, to raise money for a new ship. This was an assignment from which he cringed, for there was no collaboration with the church in Australia, and nobody knew he was coming. "With unaffected reluctance, I at last felt constrained to this unwelcome but apparently inevitable task," he wrote. He

found a sandalwood ship that gave him a most distressing journey to Sydney. He knew not a soul in Sydney.

He wandered lonely and disconsolate. He went to the churches, but neither ministers nor anyone else took any interest in him. Then one Sunday afternoon he attended a children's meeting, and after the minister spoke he asked if he could speak to the children. Paton was given fifteen minutes. From here his story spread to other churches, and he was offered pulpits throughout the city and country. Money came in, and a large oil painting hanging in the Assembly Hall in Melbourne testifies to his influence on the Presbyterian Church in Australia. A ship of 159 tons was bought in Sydney and named *Dayspring II*. The name was borrowed from Luke 1:78: "The dayspring from on high hath visited us." With this ship Paton was able to revisit his beloved islands.

In his autobiography, Paton recalls his first baptism and communion for native converts from cannibalism, held after twelve months' testing their faith. "At the moment when I put the bread and wine into those dark hands, once stained with the blood of cannibalism, now stretched out to receive and partake of the emblems and seal of the Redeemer's love, I had a foretaste of the joy of Glory."

CHAPTER 4

ADVENTISTS JOIN THE ASSAULT ON HEATHENISM

"O to see a missionary and a Christian teacher planted on every island of the New Hebrides! For this I labor and pray," wrote John G. Paton after being driven out of Tanna with much suffering and loss. He little dreamed that reinforcements would come through the Seventh-day Adventist mission program. Here was an answer to his prayer, as C. H. Parker and Harold Carr were sent to the New Hebrides. They came not to compete but to contribute; to make an Adventist contribution to the cause of Christian civilization in these crying islands. These men were of the same caliber as those who had paved the way. They would add their light to the flickering torch in heathen darkness and penetrate where no light had previously been.

The cordial relationship between the Adventists and their Presbyterian brethren was in the best Christian tradition. Parker wrote in glowing terms of the work of these Presbyterians who had first invaded these islands with the Christian faith. They took the brunt of the first assault, and a number of their front-line men and women died. Parker wrote to the *Australasian Record* in 1912:

> After a pleasant voyage of four nights and three days from Norfolk Island, Brother Carr and I arrived in Vila (Island of Efate), New Hebrides. Vila is built on the shoreline of two bays. Two islands, Iririki and Fila, lie in the bay; on the first is the British resident's house and the Presbyterian Hospital; on the other is the Presbyterian native school. There are . . . a thousand French residents in the group, while the English number three hundred.

> This is a condominium government, the group being governed by British and French conjointly. I was shown through the . . . hospital erected in memory of the Rev. John G. Paton. Dr. Crombie seems to be a man who understands his work and keeps things well in hand. Above all he gives the impression that he knows his God and feels with his people.
>
> While at the hospital I met Dr. Robertson, Presbyterian missionary on Erromango. He has labored there some thirty years. We had a good visit together and one which I enjoyed very much. Such ministers as these are worthy of special respect.

The first problem on entering a new field such as the New Hebrides is where to locate. The group of islands stretches some four hundred miles from north to south. On which one should they establish a base? How could they best cooperate with those already in the field? Where would they serve to the best advantage? What was the best approach, and how could they penetrate into untouched heathenism? This was a critical decision to make, and Edwin Butz, who had spent eleven years in Tonga, joined C. H. Parker and Harold Carr in their search and vital choice.

It was midyear 1912 when these pioneer missionaries established the headquarters of the Adventist mission on the small island of Atchin, separated from Malekula by only a quarter mile of sea. Here they purchased a property of twelve acres with a house and outbuildings for £150 (US$600). The property was a trading station owned by a Frenchman. He had returned home on one occasion, having been away on business, and found his wife's body lying in the front room. She had been murdered by two local natives who then fled to Malekula. Five years later they were caught and imprisoned. The trader could not live on Atchin any longer and sold it to the missionaries a few years later. When missionary Andrew Stewart paid a courtesy visit on a government officer, the officer told him, "In Atchin are the worst people in the group. You will do well if you make any impression on these people in twenty years!"

Edwin Butz reported,

> The natives are anxious for us to locate here, though they are all heathen. The Catholics carried on a work here for some years without results, and the Presbyterians have had a teacher there for four years, but the people will have nothing to do with him in the way of attending his meetings. The one white trader on the island is anxious for us to locate there. He said, "I want to live by the side of honest neighbors." A missionary doctor on an island three miles away said, "There is plenty of room and plenty to do for us all."

The property contains a house with iron roof and limed walls; with four large rooms and four small rooms. There is a verandah back and front, also outbuildings that can be used till the work warrants something better.

LIVING IN CANNIBAL COUNTRY

In those days when a missionary went to live on one of the heathen islands, he was confronted by a culture that was crude and cruel. Women were the worst victims. They had no freedom, no choice as to whom to marry, no option between life or death. This is all dictated by her husband, who bought her for a few pigs when she was still a young girl. At the age of five she began to weed in the garden. At eight or nine she had her two front teeth knocked out and was married. If she objected, she was ruthlessly beaten. If she ran away, she could have her feet or the backs of her knees burned with a hot stone, which might cripple her for life.

Women, the aged, and the sick were regarded as inferior because of weakness. The sick and aged unable to care for themselves were sometimes buried alive in shallow graves, while friends and relatives wailed and screamed to drown the cries and groans of their loved ones. Beating and sacrificing of women and girls caused an imbalance of sexes in the heathen state, and this in turn caused murders and wars, as the men fought over the surviving women. Many men had two or more wives, depending upon their ability to buy them with pigs. Polygamy also caused much quarreling among the women. John G. Paton told of a chief he knew whose wives lived in jealousy of each other. While he was away at war with his son, the favorite, a tall, powerful woman, armed herself with an axe and murdered the others. On his return he made peace with her and, perhaps from fear, promised to protect her against revenge.

On becoming a Christian, natives were required to put away all wives but one. This was an obstacle, but sincere converts made the sacrifice. Paton tells of one chief who put ten of his eleven wives away, thus testifying to his conversion. In fact, the missionary said, it was no hardship for the women. Since men outnumbered women, the women released were soon chosen by waiting men.

"Three women came screaming into our house for us to protect them from their husbands who were about to kill them," Paton once wrote. "We dare not even plead for them, so we were told, for these raging savages would kill us immediately." John Geddie almost lost his life this way, without saving the woman from being strangled. "A savage gave his poor wife a beating just before our house, and in front of our eyes, while we in vain strove to prevent it. Such scenes

were common, and no one thought of interfering. Even if she died, neighbors took little notice of it. The girls, with their mothers, have to toil and slave in the village plantation. They must prepare all the materials for fencing these around, to bear every burden, and be knocked about at will by men and boys."

The lot of a heathen boy was quite different. His education was to aim skillfully with a bow, to throw a spear faultlessly at a mark, to wield powerfully the club and tomahawk, and to shoot well with a musket when he could obtain one. He accompanied his father on all wars and preparations for war, and was initiated into all cruelties and lusts as the very prerequisites of his being regarded as a man and warrior.

IMPOSSIBLE EMPLOYEES

The hiring of native labor on the island of Atchin proved to be a problem. As Mrs. Parker was the main teacher at the school, and more than occupied, she might employ native women and girls to do her chores. Besides, by this means she could train them in cleanliness and orderliness. Mrs. Stewart wrote,

> Lately we have tried hard to get help in our homes, but only after many attempts, failures and disappointments did we at last persuade a woman to come regularly to wash. She was progressing, so that she knew enough not to boil black socks with white shirts; but without warning she ceased coming and cannot be persuaded to return.
>
> Girls are not available because when quite young they are sold. A young woman came to work and was doing well, when her husband turned up and wanted to know why she was working. "You know, Missus, I paid pigs for her, and when a woman has a husband she does not need to work elsewhere, she must stay home." We tried to employ two young girls, but after two days they refused to do anything but weed the garden.

So the teachers had to do their own chores, adding to their already full program.

LANGUAGE AND LITERACY

Language was also an acute problem. Geddie tells that the natives were shy about giving away their language and had to be bribed with ship's biscuits to tell the meaning of sounds they made. Think of it! No characters, no written language, no teachers, grammar, syntax, rules—just sounds from which the foreigner had to extract meaning before they could converse with the people. Yet the Reverend

Powell was able to preach in the Aneityumese language in four weeks, and John Geddie in six weeks. Geddie remarked, "We consider ourselves the most intellectual people on earth, but these South Sea Islanders will smile at our stupidity about many things, in which we are inferior to them." Parker wrote,

> The condition of these islanders has been unfavorable to the development of their mental energy. Nevertheless, there are indications of a fair amount of mental power among them. They have mythology, which though absurd and false, is at least ingenious. They have their historical traditions which are transmitted from generation to generation. They can express their thoughts in a humorous manner, and often in figures of speech, forcible and appropriate. Their language, too, is copious. Many speak two or more languages.
>
> Like most rude tribes, they show that cultivation of the powers of observation which renders them in their own sphere so superior to civilized men. They recognize every footprint they see, and of every fowl or pig they can name the owner.

Someone might be hidden in the bush, said Parker, when one of his party would call out. An answer would come back from the distance, naming the individual who had spoken and telling where that person was going. "I was astonished," he said, "and asked them how they knew. I heard no footsteps, but they heard and also recognized whose footsteps they were."

CHAPTER 5

PROBING MYSTERIOUS MALEKULA

Two years and three months had passed since Parker and Carr and their wives had commenced mission work in the New Hebrides. The Union Conference was in session, and C. H. Parker was called to give a report on the progress of the island mission. He told how most of their time was occupied with restoring buildings, making thousand-gallon tanks to catch water from the roof, renewing termite-eaten floors, and other tasks. "The Lord's hand," he said,

> has especially guided in this base. It is virgin soil, and is an open door to the great population of Malekula. Santo, the next island of large population, is forty miles away, Ambrym sixty, Aoba and Pentecost about the same, and Epi only eighty miles. So our mission is in close proximity to the bulk of the population of the New Hebrides. At present we run all missionary operations on Atchin, as the Presbyterians have taken away their two native teachers on account of the massacre of their workers on Malekula; for they charged the Atchin people with being the instigators.
>
> The old Copra house has been well restored, painted and given windows and doors, a rostrum and seats. We dedicated it as a church and school on January 17, 1914. Mrs. Parker does most of the teaching, and at present has eighteen pupils. Those who have been regular in attendance are doing good work. Attendance on Sabbath is about nineteen.

> The natives take a great interest in singing from *Christ in Song*, often holding it upside down.

Just two months after this report was given, the Carrs lost their little boy through sickness, and the parents had to return to Australia because of serious illness. This was a sad situation for the Parkers. Now alone on the island, they had to adjust their program both in the mission work on Atchin and in reaching out to other islands. The nearest island, Malekula, became the great gospel challenge to Parker, now the itinerant Adventist missionary for the whole group.

To a missionary serving these islands, a launch is even more necessary than a car in the homeland. Without it he is confined, even stranded. This was the position of these missionaries for two years. Little wonder that they harassed the union conference, who communicated the urgency to H. M. Ford, the boat builder of Sydney with whom they had placed the order. At last, on April 30, 1914, a rugged little vessel of twenty-six feet with a beam of nine feet was ready for delivery. Besides a five-horsepower engine she had sails; with a fair wind she could attain a speed of eight knots. From the foremast a "coach house" extended twelve feet back, under which the engine was situated, with a bunk on either side. The cockpit at the stern, seating ten, was covered with a neat awning. After inspection, the launch ran across the Sydney harbor, where the ship *Marsian* was berthed, and was hauled aboard to be delivered to the Atchin Adventist Mission.

The launch proved a tremendous boon to Parker. His burning ambition was to reach out into the unknown, to invade heathenism in the raw, particularly on Malekula. This large island, some sixty miles long by twenty-five wide, was only a quarter of a mile away from Atchin.

ISLAND OF FEAR

From Atchin, C. H. Parker wrote to the *Australasian Record*:

> Sunday, February 22, 1914, was a sad day for the Presbyterian mission in this district. Just a few miles from our mission, five of their native teachers were shot, roasted, and eaten. The following Wednesday the missionary who had charge of this district came and removed his two native teachers from Atchin, telling me he did not consider it safe for them to remain, as there was a plot to kill everyone that wore calico (loincloth), and that the Atchin people were the cause of it. We are now left alone with these people. We could not leave if we wanted to, for we have no boat by which to take passage.

In a previous letter, Parker had written, "The trader and his family had to flee, as there was a plot formed to take his life; in fact they said that all the white people had to go. But your missionaries have dwelt in the secret place of the Most High . . ."

Constant dangers added to the burdens of the Parkers, now left alone under the shadows of cannibalism. He was urgently advised to leave the island because of danger from the savage element. He wrote to Australia: "Our lot for the present seems to be cast amongst the unpleasant things of life, but this must be best for us, and for the work of the Lord here. We have no fears. Our trust is in the One who holds the universe in His hands." His life was threatened a number of times, and for twelve months he and his wife labored alone; she with her teaching, and he itinerating on Malekula, probing the possibilities of another mission outpost.

With the new launch, Parker was no longer marooned. During his first foray into Malekula he had made friends with a coastal chief who spoke pidgin English, and was he familiar with the traders. Parker asked to be taken back to the wild bush people in the secluded hills. The chief replied, "No, Missi Parker, you no game, you frighten. Him wild fella." "You try me," said Parker. "I'll go with you." Finally, after some persuasion, the nervous chief agreed to take him back, and arrangements were to meet on the shore early one Sunday morning.

When Parker met the chief, the native man had a bodyguard, spears, clubs, and muskets. Anxious, yet apprehensive, Parker followed the instruction of the chief to keep close and follow his footsteps immediately. They set off on a long trek into the interior, where white men had probably never gone. The chief made his own special whistling signal as he went along. When they met natives along the way, they would stop while the bodyguard surrounded the chief and Parker. After a parley they would pass on through grass ten feet tall, but always onward and upward into the mysterious region where there was no knowing what kind of reception awaited them.

After some hours they arrived at a village of the Big Nambus. The coastal chief now lost control, and the man-eaters of Malekula took over. Fierce and formidable, but obviously intrigued with this pasty-skinned curiosity, they took hold of Parker, pulled aside his clothing where they could, and examined his body to see if he was put together the same way as they. There seemed to be no hostility—but no warmth either. There were no smiles, only cold, watchful stares. The nature of the heathen is to ignore rather than respond to warmth.

Parker kept his eyes alert for those who were sick or had wounds or sores. Finding several, he gave simple treatments with bandages and medicine. Unable to speak their language, he occupied himself in this way and tried to let them know he was not there to hurt them but to help. Having run out of bandages

and medicine, and feeling he had spent long enough with them, he closed his kit bag, moved back to join his friendly chief, and waved his hand in farewell to these savages who had neither welcomed him nor eaten him. He was still left wondering what they thought of the "plenty white man."

Atchin was only a little better. A government officer had warned both C. H. Parker and A. G. Stewart that Atchin, the island chosen for Adventist mission headquarters, had proved one of the worst islands for the murders of whites. "You can never civilize these people, let alone make Adventists of them," warned the officer. However, Parker ignored the warning, feeling that he was gradually winning their confidence, though the going was slow.

Then a French trader came their way, selling the people liquor and carousing all night with them. "Many had to be carried home, while others were left lying around in the bush," Parker reported.

> The night was filled with their frenzied cries and outbursts. We could not sleep, so spent much of the night in prayer. Next morning the trader came to renew former acquaintance. But I gave him to understand that such work as he was doing found no answering chord of friendship in our hearts, and that he was an enemy of the people rather than a friend. I wanted the natives to see how we regarded drink and those that sold it.
>
> On Sunday morning I called all the people together, and they came with few exceptions. I spoke to them on the evils of liquor drinking, then read to them what God says about it, and closed my remarks by pointing out that they had the power to prevent liquor from being sold on the island, just as they had the power to let it come in. I told them to go away and talk it over among themselves. This they did. A little later a number came and told me that they had decided not to touch grog again, and if the trader came they would tell him to take his things and go. The trader came back in a week expecting to do as before. He came firing off a blast of dynamite. The people sold him a large amount of copra [dried coconut kernels], but not a penny did they spend on drink. He taunted them, but they told him they had "savied finished." They told him not to bring his grog ashore, and if he did he must take his things and go. The trader came a third time, but they remained true to their decision.

The natives were in serious trouble with the government over the murder and cannibalism of the teachers mentioned earlier. Both British and French warships appeared to subdue the culprits. Soldiers and police followed the trails of the Big Nambus cannibals into the mountains. In home territory the natives

fled to their familiar haunts, where they readily ambushed the soldiers, killing five, plus three native policemen and a teacher. One of the native policemen and the teacher had to be left in the bush, and their bodies were eaten. Only one bushman was killed and another taken prisoner. Missionary Parker wrote,

> The heathen are jubilant. They are boasting that they have beaten the combined forces of Britain and France.
>
> Shortly after the failure of this expedition, a delegation from these two villages of bushmen came down to us and asked us to mediate for them. The *H.M.S. Torch* called two weeks later, and we had the privilege of arranging a meeting between the commander and this people. We brought all of the people from these two villages down from the mountains to our mission house, and here they conferred together. Everything was settled up satisfactorily, and the people gave surety of keeping the peace by promising five pounds, which they have already placed in our hands for the *Torch* when she returns. We cannot speak too highly of Captain I. R. LeHunte Ward, Commander of the *Torch*. He had no desire to slaughter the natives, but thought the more peaceful way was to get them together to talk the matter over. Thus a wide door is open to us among the bush people. Their coming to us shows that they have learned we are their friends.

With these developments on Atchin and Malekula, Missionary Parker appealed to the union conference for suitable assistance in the work that was now growing to larger proportions, particularly on Malekula. There were exciting days ahead for the mission in the New Hebrides.

CHAPTER 6

NORMAN AND ALMA WILES

Norman Wiles, of Adelaide, South Australia, was a young man in his early twenties when C. H. Parker visited Avondale College and told of his adventures on the islands. With his mother and sister Vida, Norman had accepted the Adventist message some years earlier. He was good missionary material—sincere, dedicated, a Christian gentleman, and determined to devote his life to the Lord Jesus Christ. He was warm and friendly, loved by his fellow students, and esteemed as a young leader of promise.*

Alma Bernice Butz was born in Benicia, near San Francisco, California, on September 23, 1894. Her parents were called to high mission adventure in the islands of the South Pacific, setting sail on the fourth voyage of the new mission ship *Pitcairn*. Taking Alma, then a babe in arms, they boarded this two-masted brigantine of about one hundred tons' burden on May 1, 1895, with Captain Graham. There were seventeen on board, including missionary children, all bound for various islands. It took about one month to reach Pitcairn Island.

Here Edwin and Florence Butz, with their baby, disembarked to minister

* I knew Norman Wiles well and admired his Christian stature. I was also well acquainted with Alma Butz. Edwin Butz, her father, when president of the Tasmanian Conference, visited our church and our home many times when I was a small boy. He also called me into the ministry when I graduated in 1920, so that under his blessing I made my first fumbling efforts to find my feet in this divine vocation. Like others, I followed closely the calling of Norman and Alma to the New Hebrides and shared the shock of the tragedy on Malekula. Many years later, during Alma's convalescence, it was my privilege to visit her and talk over her early years.

to the community. Eighty persons had been baptized four years earlier, on the first voyage of the *Pitcairn*. Now Butz was to strengthen the faith of this island church, the very essence of isolation. Here Alma had her first birthday. Her mother used to tie the toddler with a long rope to the clothesline, so that she had a fair amount of playground yet was prevented from running too close to the high cliffs holding back the sea.

When Alma was twenty months old, the *Pitcairn* called again and took the family to Tonga. For ten years, Nuku'alofa, the capital of Tonga, was Alma's growing-up place. Here her father joined E. Hilliard in evangelism, while Mrs. Butz engaged in medical work. They adopted a young girl, Maria Young, who became part of the household. Then a stranger, Ned Edwards, an Englishman, was brought to their house one day. He had been shipwrecked and stranded on an island. Natives had caught him and tied him to a tree, holding him as the main entrée of a cannibal feast in preparation. Fortunately, a boat's crew came upon him, cut him loose, and took him to Nuku'alofa, where he was taken to the Butzes' house. He proved to be of honorable character. He accepted the Adventist message and apparently was a great favorite of Alma's. She said that to leave him behind in Tonga when they were called away was one of saddest memories of her girlhood. Later, he married Maria Young, the Butzes' adopted girl.

Butz was called to New Zealand for a time, then to Wahroonga, Australia, and later to Adelaide, where Alma met Norman Wiles. Both were in their teens, both had been raised in a Christian atmosphere, and a wholesome friendship began. Later both found themselves students at Australasian Missionary College. Their friendship deepened, though college rules in those days were very restrictive for couples. Anything approaching courtship was not for the college campus. An imaginary line was drawn through the chapel right to the boundaries of the extensive college property, including rivers and forest country—one side was called the "Boys' Walk" and the other side the "Girls' Walk." Woe to any boy or girl who lacked a legitimate excuse for trespassing on the wrong side of the imaginary line!

For Norman and Alma these rules were not needed. Their moral and spiritual standards were evident in their deportment. In fact, at this time one could hardly detect a serious relationship between them.

Near the end of 1914, the Gore Hill Park camp meeting was held near Sydney. Alma and her parents were settled in a comfortable tent, partitioned across the middle. At this time, Parker, who was visiting Australia from the New Hebrides, thrilled the congregation with his exciting adventures. There was also a union conference committee meeting, in which both Parker and Butz were involved. Alma later reminisced,

> After this meeting I was in the back of the tent, and my parents were sitting in the front in serious conversation. I heard my name coming through strongly. They were discussing the possibility that Norman and I might marry and go out to the islands. I listened intently, now, for this was a new idea to me. I felt resentful, for I had not been consulted, and Norman had not mentioned matrimony. It was *my* business, and no one was going to rob me of my independence. I would not submit to arrangements made without my knowing it. I would not be bought or sold by committee action—so there! I slipped out of the tent and went for a walk.
>
> On my return father was not there, but Norman was, in deep conversation with mother. I sat in the back of the tent for a while, still boiling inside. Then I set out on another walk. Mother spotted me and called me back. After telling me some things about the committee action, she left so that Norman and I could talk the matter out between ourselves. We talked over the advisability and the future possibilities at some length. Norman never proposed in the usual way. We simply felt that if this was the action of the committee, the Lord was leading and that settled the matter.

A month later the couple was married. After spending a few months at the Sydney Sanitarium to acquire some knowledge of simple medicine, both eagerly boarded the ship for the New Hebrides. Their destination was Atchin, where they shared the headquarters house with the Parkers. The house had been divided for this purpose.

A DIFFERENT KIND OF OPPOSITION

The Atchinese people seemed pleased to welcome this attractive young couple to their island. However, another young man arrived on the island about the same time and attracted the favorable attention of the people. He was a graduate from a prominent university, having majored in ethnology and anthropology. An agnostic, he discouraged the natives from leaving their heathen ways and accepting Christianity.

The people were both flattered and confused by this white man's instruction. He even bribed them to repeat some of their traditional heathen practices that they had abandoned. Of course, it was much easier to slip back into heathen ways than to change to Christian moral standards.

This man spent almost a year on Atchin. While the missionaries looked on anxiously, many returned to their devil worship. This meant preparation for a

war also, which grew so serious that it threatened the scientist himself. According to Parker, the man fled to the mission house and implored the missionary to "quench the flames of murder which he had wickedly started."

Norman and Alma Wiles had walked out to watch the heathen dance but were soon hurried back by friendly natives. Guns, stones, and clubs were in the hands of all. The island was divided into two parties, and furious challenges were flying back and forth. Parker stood between the warring parties, holding the clubs of the leaders and remonstrating with them. For nearly two hours he wrestled and reasoned and prayed. Every moment it seemed that the fight would begin; but though weakened by fever and by this grueling effort, he managed to hold the leaders at bay till the cry went up, *"Esu, esu, kap mul, kap mul"* ("Finished, go home").

Conditions continued to be unsettled for some time, and frequently the missionary was called to settle heathen quarrels.

Despite the setback, not all the natives followed the professor's philosophy. About thirty still held to their faith in the Christian God and attended Sabbath services. Mrs. Parker also held meetings around the island for women especially, and she was rewarded to see a changed attitude toward the mission, as at last smiles lighted up sullen faces.

CHAPTER 7

FIRST MISSION ON MALEKULA

After the Atchinese had flirted with a return to devil worship and fratricidal war, they began to return to the Christian school and meetings. The missionaries took courage and resumed their full program.

But there remained the challenge of Malekula, a grim, heathen Goliath with his axe and musket defying the Christian David, armed with his Bible and picture roll. Where to begin? Parker had made forays into the island, testing the mood of the people and holding meetings. He even held meetings at Lalip, where the Presbyterian teachers had been murdered, though this proved too dangerous to continue. The only way to achieve permanent results was to establish a mission and live among the people. Norman reported,

> Choosing a favorable day and accompanied by some Atchin boys, we set sail for Matanavat, a native village twenty miles around the West coast of Malekula. It was a two-hour run, but we were cautious about landing, as this was the place where the bushmen had threatened to come down and shoot us. The local people however, are friendly, and we were soon shaking hands with them and getting acquainted. The chief wanted to come back with us, so we brought him. On our return we passed another village we wanted to visit, but the shore was all solid rock. The people were friendly but reticent; however, they came out and brought us by canoe. We had an hour's visit, but thought we would have to swim to the launch, for it was a long time before an attempt was made to take us. It was not easy launching their canoe over the rocks.

The Matanavat chief welcomed the mission people and offered them a good site with a promise to clear the land and put up a building for the school. These people were friendly with the wild bushmen, and through these villagers Wiles had hopes of making contact with those savages. The bush people were always wandering around with loaded muskets, either looking for trouble or making it.

Norman commented, "We believe the Lord is going before us to open the way to these islands. He is very near to us out here, and has blessed us with health and strength, while all around us we see much sickness." A few months later he wrote of the progress at Matanavat:

> The boys of Matanavat have worked well at clearing the bush off the mission land, but as they are busy planting yams they have not been able to put up our school. At present we hold our services under a tree, using mother earth as seats. They are just learning the alphabet and some of the simplest words. The houses are worse here than on Atchin. One hole is generally left by which the owner crawls inside. They look like large dog kennels.
>
> Away up in the hill country are a wild people known as the Big Nambus, and they have never had a missionary of any kind among them. The Lord has given us access to these people, and we want to go right in and work for them. They have a powerful chief who is in favor of the mission, and they want us to come. We may have mentioned before a place called Lalip, where Pastor Parker has been going to hold services. All was going well until trouble sprang up among the people, and word came that bushmen were lying in wait to kill the missionary. Other warnings have come also, so for the time being the meetings have been dropped. Still we are praying that the Lord will open the doors again and allow us to continue to bring them the Gospel.

Some weeks after this report, the slow-moving natives got busy on the church and meetinghouse, building it of bush material after their custom but guided by the missionary. Then Wiles and Parker, with native help, hauled timber and corrugated iron around to Matanavat and built a simple house for Norman and Alma, a one-room dwelling eight by ten feet with a large verandah to catch all possible breezes and accommodate visiting natives. Missionaries in pioneering days had to be practical. Rarely did they have a house to live in till they built one. They might persuade natives to lend a hand, but they were the only ones who knew how to put sawn timber and iron together to make an acceptable dwelling. The natives could cut poles, brace them together, and cover them with plaited grass and leaves. But the white man wanted something more substantial

in a climate where rain was prolific and hurricane-force winds blew.

In these malaria-infested islands, the human body can take only so much. It was time for the Parkers to be replaced by another experienced couple. So an exchange was made with Pastor and Mrs. A. G. Stewart of Fiji.

Before the Parkers left for Fiji, they decided to take Norman around the coast some thirty miles to make contact with the Big Nambus, whom Parker had met once earlier in their mountain village. He and Norman knew this trip would be venturesome and dangerous.

Alma Wiles recalls the night before her husband left on this hazardous journey. They discussed the perils of unpredictable cannibals and the rocky coast. Then together they prayed for divine guidance and protection. In the morning it was raining heavily, the wind was blowing, the sea was rough, and the clouds all but obscured the coastline. They had second thoughts. Maybe it would be wise to postpone the venture till the weather improved. They had morning prayer and opened the Bible to find a message from the Lord. The Book opened to Ecclesiastes 11:4: "He that observeth the wind shall not sow; and he that regardeth the clouds shall not reap." That settled it. The missionaries kissed their wives farewell, boarded their little craft, and steered into the wind and storm. For hours their launch made its way through the crests and troughs of a choppy sea. At last there was a break in the clouds and a lull in the wind along the Big Nambus coast, and they could see land. They headed straight toward the shore, where a number of spectators lined the beach. What kind of welcome awaited them?

By previous arrangement, Norman was to remain on the launch so as to be alert for help and a getaway if needed. Parker, conscious of the promise, "Lo, I am with you always, even unto the end of the world," stepped into his dinghy and rowed toward the sullen figures awaiting him.

As Parker arrived on shore he found himself surrounded by thirty of the fiercest-looking savages he had ever seen. They were nude except for a bark belt around the waist, to which was attached a bunch of bark fiber rolled around the groin. The savages were armed and hideously painted. In a few moments they led him away from the sandy beach to a cliff where, under an overhanging rock, they seated him upon a stone. They brought some broad leaves of the banana tree, which they held over him to shelter him from the rain. The chief himself did not come to meet him, but he sent his brother, who attempted to converse with Parker. Though this was difficult, they were able to make themselves understood.

On these occasions Parker always made a feature of his medical bag. If language was a barrier, the bag was a boon, an object of mystery and focus of interest. How neatly it opened its mouth to show its contents! Most had never seen

such a bag, let alone bandages, bottles, and ointments, which Parker applied to their many sores, wounds, and ills. They soon discovered that he was there to help and to heal.

The chief had not come because he was under a taboo, a tribal restriction that confined him to his home for a number of days. Nothing definite could be arranged without the chief, so Parker promised to come again, travel into the bush country, and visit the chief. He was able to let the people know why he had come—to inquire whether they wanted a mission among them. As the reply was favorable, he promised to return. Waving good-bye, he made his way back to the launch, where Norman anxiously waited.

Before he left for Fiji, Parker again visited the Big Nambus country. The people's friendliness toward the missionaries seemed to be genuine. The head chief, Nikambat, was an amiable old savage, and from Parker's first visit to the mountain village, the old man manifested an almost affectionate friendship. With a promise of protection and land for a mission and school, he tried to persuade Pastor Parker to come and live there.

PASTOR A. G. STEWART TAKES OVER

When the Stewarts arrived in the New Hebrides in February 1916, they found conditions more primitive than they had known anywhere else. The people were practically naked at all times. He wrote,

> The influence of nudity is degrading. But in attempting to change the customs of the native peoples one must be extremely careful. It is unwise and unsafe to appear to command. The savages have never been subjected to discipline. New Year's Eve we entertained them on the verandah of the mission house by the use of magic lantern pictures, showing pictures of Australia and of other peoples of the islands in the South Seas, all dressed in clean shirts and loin cloths. I told them that I had a request to make: when they came upon the mission property, to attend school or church services or as visitors, they would please put some form of covering on their bodies.
>
> It was most pleasing to us when two of the leading men agreed to do so. By way of a reminder, we tied a piece of red calico around the gate-post, They seldom needed reminding of this rule. And even before they had opportunity to secure the necessary calico, some came clothed in the most ludicrous fashion. One old man came in a heavy overcoat reaching to his ankles, and it was a hot tropical day. Another just held an ordinary

> sack around his loins. When we received cases of clothing from Australia they were unable to distinguish between male and female garments, and sometimes they came dressed in clothes of the opposite sex.

Also during their first year, the Stewarts were compelled to realize the horrors of cannibalism on Malekula. The trading steamer, when it called at Atchin, brought news that an Australian family sixteen miles south of Atchin had been murdered. It appeared that the father had just finished his evening meal and had carried a chair outside the house to sit quietly and smoke his pipe when bushmen from twelve miles inland approached. They surrounded him, and without warning he was clubbed from behind and instantly killed. His family of six were found around the table murdered in cold blood. The body of the oldest boy, a fine lad of thirteen, was carried away for a cannibal feast. Human flesh was sent to several villages and received with the understanding that at some future time the gift must be repaid in flesh of the same kind.

Opposite the Atchin mission headquarters on Malekula, a native had been shot while feeding his chickens. Some treacherous savage shot him without any apparent reason, as this was the way of the bushmen.

This meant immediate war between the tribes involved; and as Andrew Stewart had commenced mission work in this particular village on Malekula, holding Sabbath services regularly, he was in a dilemma as to whether he should risk entering this war zone. He wrote in his report, "Every step of advancement on murderous Malekula has been made only with great courage in the midst of constant exposure to danger, and courage must not fail now, lest one of the few open doors should be closed."

The natives on Atchin showed serious concern for his safety, urging him to abandon the idea of going that Sabbath. "Head belong bushmen he cranky. Suppose he look one man, he shoot. He no care nothing." Some natives went around to the kitchen and interviewed Mrs. Stewart: "Missus, you no let master he go long bush long morning. Manbush he stop no good. He walk about, he look out men, suppose he look missionary, he shoot, he no care. Head belong him he cranky too much."

But Stewart went, appealing for divine protection. Making his way some five miles into the Malekula bush, he was relieved by the welcome the natives gave him. They listened to his message, but as he was leaving they urged him not to return to their village till conditions were more settled and they had avenged the murder of their friend.

CHAPTER 8

THE PARKERS DEPART

A month after the mission house at Matanavat was finished, the Parkers packed their belongings and boarded the ship *Makambo,* which was to take them away from their hard-won mission achievements in the New Hebrides. The sorrow in parting with their cannibal friends and transformed natives comes through in his final report, written June 2, 1916, on board ship:

> On April 26 we completed our Matanavat house, and on that day Brother and Sister Wiles moved in. It was a new experience for them to be alone, but they shouldered their responsibilities with true Christian fortitude. The next morning Brother Wiles made another visit to the Big Nambus. This people met us with greater friendliness than before. Hardly a musket could be seen. They had the place cleared for the church building, and a number of the posts cut. I surveyed the land for registration. We had taken six acres, and they say we can have as much land as we wish. I held a service for them and they seemed to have lost their fearfulness. They sat down close to me with their faces looking up into mine. They were eager at the close to see more of the pictures and to know what they mean. It was hard to leave them.
>
> With satisfaction we returned to Matanavat, where I left Brother Wiles and went to Atchin. A note was handed to me by Sister Wiles: "Dear Brother Parker, I have spent the afternoon with the women in their town, and they are so glad that we are to stay with them. I am so happy." Sabbath

was a good day for us on Atchin, and inland on Malekula. I visited Lalip again, and a number gathered for service. At nine o'clock at night we were made so glad to see Brother and Sister A. G. Stewart, who have come to take charge of the work in the New Hebrides. Most of the islanders gathered on the beach to tender them a welcome.

The days that followed were busy ones as we visited Matanaat, a number of coastal towns, and two towns inland, so that Brother Stewart might come into personal touch with every place where we have labored. We visited the Big Nambus again. They want their missionary settled among them. When I told the chief that I would be leaving for Fiji, he put his arm around me and gave me a big hug, saying, "You savvy come back again, Mr. Parker. You savvy him place belong you. You walk about here among me fellow. You friend belong me fellow; me friend belong you." I told him that Mr. Wiles was to be their missionary. They seemed to take to him.

The *Makambo* called for us May 23. Our first night aboard was a struggle for each of us, and as we saw the last faint lines of Atchin passing from our view, we could understand something of how Joseph felt, when he gazed for the last time on the ridge of hills, at the foot of which his father's tent was erected. However, God knows best, so we leave it all in the hands of Him Who feels our heart pangs. We ask the united prayers of our people for Brother and Sister Stewart, as they direct the work in the New Hebrides. They will meet many discouragements and will need the faith of Caleb. Especially we ask you to pray for Brother and Sister Wiles as they locate among the Big Nambus. This move will be fraught with a great deal of danger, as they are the worst cannibals of the New Hebrides. One false step may mean his death.

After the Parkers had gone, Norman and Alma sensed a load of responsibility resting on them. Here was Malekula, an island some sixty miles long and twenty-five wide, inhabited by thousands of primitive people, separated into many independent tribes and speaking a variety of languages. They ranged from the peaceful on one side of the island to warlike cannibals on the other.

It hadn't been long since the demise of the five Presbyterian teachers, and hostile emotions were still high among the natives. Norman's life, too, was threatened. A white man had been murdered by two natives from a certain tribe, after which there had been a government expedition. A number of natives were killed, including the brother of the chief of the offending tribe, but the two murderers escaped. The chief, breathing revenge, vowed to eat nothing until he had feasted on the flesh of a white man. Norman was the only white

man available, and the chief gave the previous murderers cartridges to shoot the missionary. They came near to Norman's house, but some friendly natives who happened to be shooting at birds scared off the would-be murderers. Norman learned this from natives from another tribe whom the men met on their way home from their uncompleted errand.

Matanavat, with its hastily constructed Australian type of house, was the first home Norman and Alma had to themselves. Without amenities such as kitchen and bathroom, it was no showpiece, except as an example of a pioneer house. At least they could shut themselves in from prying eyes, and Alma had no complaints; she and Norman were young and adventuresome. They moved from village to village, looking, learning, and discovering new people, languages, customs, and practices—always endeavoring to capture the interest of the natives and introduce to them the gospel. Above all, they sought to show kindness, love, and trust—traits foreign to the heathen culture.

Norman held school and worship services daily with those anxious to learn. He did not try to learn all the languages, but concentrated on one while Alma learned another. Since those who lived near the coast understood pidgin English, he used it while he worked on reducing their sounds to an alphabet and creating a writing system for them. In a report to Australia, he wrote, "I have taken a census of the people of this village. There are 320. The language here extends to other villages, which is a good thing, for it is a difficult language to learn. I shall have to make a new alphabet to accommodate the sounds."

For two years Matanavat was their home. From here they attended the needs of local villages and reached out to more distant tribes, hoping ultimately to conquer the cannibals for Christ. Norman and Andrew Stewart made frequent visits to these people to maintain friendly contact. It was a trek of three to seven miles back into the mountain to reach various villages.

A NIGHT WITH THE BIG NAMBUS

Andrew G. Stewart reported a visit with the people of the Big Nambus in 1918. The Wileses had gone to Australia to recover from serious bouts with malaria, so Matanavat had no missionary for over a year. Ross James and his wife had just arrived on Atchin to join the New Hebridean team; and to serve as a teacher, Jope had come from Fiji with his wife. Stewart wrote,

> Last month we decided that Mrs. Stewart and I, accompanied by our Fijian workers, should spend a fortnight at the Matanavat Mission, leaving

Brother and Sister James to carry on the work here on Atchin. We went by launch to Matanavat, and Brother James and I decided to make a trip to the Big Nambus. A number of natives from Matanavat were going to visit the Big Nambus people, so Jope and I took passage in their boat. Having little wind, the passage was a slow one, and late in the afternoon we reached the village. We found the people busy making preparations for a big dance that evening, so it was useless to try to conduct a service until the following morning. We decided to stay overnight.

Not having planned to stay overnight, I had brought no bedding. But that may be just as well; there will be fewer things to wash after a night in one of those native houses. We were shown a "man's house," a long, narrow hut with the roof resting on the ground, and only one small opening about two feet, six inches square. As we had no light, I suggested that while it was still daylight we go in and see where we were to sleep, or rather spend the night. After we had been inside a few minutes our eyes grew accustomed to the darkness, and we discovered a large pile of hot stones in the middle of the house, upon which was lying a roasted pig. On one side was a man lying on a leaf mat on the ground, who responded to our gaze with, "Master, me sick." On the other side was a narrow bunk, consisting of about five pieces of bamboo tied together. But feeling the ridges of the bamboo and noticing that it was only about five feet long, I decided to try the earthen floor. On looking around I found two of their plaited leaf mats, which I spread on the floor where there was the least dust, and as far from the pig as I could get.

We did some visiting and treated the sick before dark. After eating a few biscuits we had brought, and having worship with the sick man in the house, we decided to retire early. We were told that people from other villages would arrive and would dance till daybreak. With my camera for a pillow I tried to rest and was nearly asleep when the yells of the approaching dances burst on our ears. Soon the tomtoms were being beaten vigorously and all sleep for the night was banished.

After a time I suggested to Jope that we get up and walk around for a while. We came to the dancing ground, and there under the flickering light of the wild-cane torches we could see the painted figures of the dancers glistening with perspiration as they gyrated and yelled, holding muskets firmly in their hands. We noticed the whites of their eyes and teeth in contrast to their black bodies.

We retired to our humble beds and awaited the cessation of the noise at break of day. When they were finished we were ready to begin. Gathering a few of the men around us who had attended services before, we started

> by singing a hymn in the Big Nambus language which Brother Wiles has translated. Then in Pidgin English I briefly told them the story of redemption, and had those near to me interpret it into their own language which the visitors understood. We used the picture rolls; they make a splendid textbook and always excite interest.

Soon afterward the missionaries laid plans to remove the Matanavat house and reerect it among the Big Nambus. This kind of labor under a tropical sun, in a fever-infested region, was very taxing on their health. But the visits to the Big Nambus were paying spiritual dividends.

The land for a mission had already been given, and the natives urged the visitors to "bring a hammer and nails next time so that we can build you a house and school." But tribal wars persisted, and the government withheld permission to let the missionaries settle there. It would be a bad reflection on the government to have more missionaries killed, roasted, and eaten as the Presbyterian teachers had been. The tragedy had triggered a gunboat confrontation with the natives, and more lives were lost.

Then came Chief Nikambat, leader of the headhunters, with a deputation of warriors to meet Mr. King, the British commissioner. Stewart reported,

> The Commissioner asked the chief a number of questions and then gave him opportunity to talk, and each time the chief made a statement it included the words, "Me fellow want missionary, he stop along me." The interview made a favorable impression upon Mr. King, and in a subsequent interview with him he asked me our plans. I told him we were ready to go ahead and build a house for Mr. Wiles. He asked me if we wanted to go right on top [of the island], and I told him we were planning to start on a lower level, and if necessary move farther in later. This plan he favored. So we left, thanking the Lord that the way is again open.
>
> We proceeded at once to erect a house for Brother and Sister Wiles upon a nice elevation about a mile from the beach and close to a place now occupied by a number of natives. This is a small but comfortable house, 24 feet by 13, with a verandah back and front. Here we expect to start work for the Nambus people and let the future determine where the permanent site of the mission will be. Already the leading men from other villages have visited the building and for the first time have looked upon sawn timber, corrugated iron, and the fair skin of the missionary carpenter.

Norman had been physically weakened by recurring bouts of fever and his strenuous efforts in a tropical climate. Alma was in better health than her husband. After four years in the tropics he spent a few months at the Sydney Sanitarium to recover his health. One Friday evening he came to the college and spoke at our Friday night service. We students were shocked as he stepped onto the rostrum. He was still a young man, blond, confident, consecrated to his task, and anxious to get back to Malekula. We marveled at his determination, but he looked pale and thin. As he approached the pulpit, he smiled at his youthful congregation, then opened his Bible to Isaiah 41:2: "Keep silence before me, O islands; and let my people renew their strength."

The impact of Norman's presence and message that night made a lasting impression on students and faculty. Norman was obviously a dedicated missionary who loved his people. The more degraded they were, the greater their need and the more sensitive he was to help them. Life might be lonely and empty of homeland comforts, but he was content to live among them, loving them with a divine affection. C. H. Watson wrote of Wiles, "Such missionaries did Norman Wiles, and his devoted wife, prove to be from their earliest days of their work. Theirs was a particularly trying service. At Matanavat they were compelled to live with a most degraded people and under peril that would test the courage of the bravest. Yet when the call came to move into even darker heathenism and cannibals, they quickly gave themselves to the more perilous undertaking."

RETURN FROM AUSTRALIA

In January 1920, Norman and Alma returned to Malekula. Their house was now in Malua Bay on the western shore of the island. Though unfinished, this house was a marked improvement on the temporary one at Matanavat. It was still some miles from Norman's parish of the bushmen cannibals of the mountains. While this meant an exhausting walk up the mountain to reach them, this was preferable to living among the Big Nambus in their home environment. To this both government and mission leaders agreed.

Norman Wiles's last report to the Australian Union Conference was published in the *Record* of May 3, 1920:

> Just now we are having an anxious time. [A local war had broken out.] Last week an old man from Tonmial, near Matanavat, blew his hand off with dynamite trying to kill fish. He was brought to us soon after, as the nearest doctor is far out of reach. We have no launch so had to do the best we could without an anesthetic. It was difficult to amputate it under these

conditions, and we are still in doubt as to how the man will fare.

Things are still unsettled here. There is no communication between the villages as they are at war. Some of the natives venture out in search of food, only to hurry home again as soon as possible. The chief of one mountain tribe was concerned about our safety, and feared lest the Amok people might shoot us. He asked some of his men to come and guard us, but as none seemed willing he came himself. We fixed them a place to sleep and they stayed three nights. We are alone again with the sick man and his companion. We were pleased that they felt responsible for our protection, although we did not feel that we needed it. These people, though numerous as yet, are dying out. Hardly any children are to be seen, not more than one to a family, and many of the men have no wives. We are just in time or there would be none left.

CHAPTER 9

ALMA'S DIARY

A few months after Norman and Alma had returned to the New Hebrides, he suffered another malarial attack and found it necessary to retreat to a more healthful area at Atchin. When word came of fighting between Nambus tribes, he forced himself to return to Malekula. Despite his weakened condition, he made his way up the mountain through the water-laden forest of ten-feet-tall grass and overhanging growth. This effort soaked him and caused his fever to return. He managed to settle a dispute between the tribes; the fighting cooled off, and soon a semblance of peace prevailed.

Now things were looking brighter, and the Wileses were getting settled in their new home. Contacts with other Nambus tribes had been achieved, resulting in calls for teachers. Clearly the love and dedication of this missionary couple had broken through to the natives' consciousness. The savages were open to Christian influence as never before. Alma said it was the happiest time of their lives on Malekula.

Now I will let Alma Wiles pick up the story in her diary:

Thursday, April 29

We planned a trip to Tonmiel, but the boat crew did not come. Instead, we went for a little trip up the coast to Man Amock's passage, gathered some shells, and returned home for dinner. However, we did not find a safe place suitable for anchoring a launch in a rough sea. Norman thought it would do me good as I had been having fever, and I did

enjoy it—it was a little break too from the monotony of days without seeing a soul.

Friday, April 30

Arranged to make the Tonmiel trip on Sunday, as we were having lovely weather. I decided not to go this time as I have been having fever. Norman rested up preparatory for his trip Sabbath. Felt feverish (a little) and remarked it was strange he always got fever the end of the week—must be Satan trying to hinder our work. He would go anyway. He asked me all through the week to go with him, but I did not feel able. I tried to get things ready for Sabbath. Norman finished the front door steps. The next week we would be settled in our new house, and how lovely it would be!

With a new launch we expect to have soon, we can do something for the Tonmiel and Matanavat people. Right now our hands are tied on account of the fighting among the Big Nambus people. Then, too, although we never talk of that side much, we will feel safer with the launch. But we are not afraid. We have never lost sleep one night because of feeling nervous, and neither of us has ever had such a feeling of protection and guidance as now. We know from experience, "The angel of the Lord encampeth round about them that fear Him, and delivereth them," and we feel sweet peace and a sense of protection. How often have murmuring thoughts been rebuked just when we were tempted to give them words. When we were out of water and both so sick that we could not get it ourselves—with no hope of anyone coming down from the village because of the fighting—along came natives, strangers from another village, who brought us some water. When it seemed we could get along no longer without some native food, along came men with what we needed. We have never before had so many instances of answered prayer.

Sabbath, May 1

Norman did not feel well in the morning but thought it only fever and he would simply come home, have an attack in the afternoon and that would be all, as had happened the week before. Everything was drenching wet so he did not start too early but finally decided to go. Had the best meeting . . . he had had for a long time. He made an appeal to them to have a regular school. . . . They finally consented and selected a piece of ground ready for Brother Stewart to see. Norman felt quite encouraged. . . . On the way home, he realized what his symptoms pointed to. When he got home, we sat on the floor by the sitting room door and he told me all. I felt anxious for we had just been studying the subject of blackwater fever

but acted as though it were nothing unusual. I prepared a hot bath for Norman and put him to bed. He had a chill that afternoon but not as bad as later. He had a fairly good night. From the start I was particular to keep his net tucked in, for my own safety as well as for his comfort. Norman told me all about his encouraging meeting first, and then ended by saying quite unconcernedly that he had fever and it was blackwater fever. Sabbath afternoon we questioned what percent of the disease was fatal.

Sunday, May 2

Seemed a bit better—urine more of a red color. He did wish that Brother Stewart would come, but would not let me send. Stewarts would think we were too fond of sending around. Natives came to work Sunday—finished the kitchen walls and cleared some of the grass so as to get rid of the swarms of mosquitoes. Sunday afternoon worse chills, sudden rise and fall in temperature, vomiting. I was up several times that night. Temperature over 105 degrees F.

Monday, May 3

I washed the clothes, but it took me till eight o'clock that night to finish. I was in and out, checking on Norman all the time. He wanted me to stay with him, but I had to wash and everything went wrong—sticks burnt out under the copper of boiling water. Poor Norman vomiting all the time, and suffering from chills—"Oh Alma, pray for me or I'll be gone, I can't stand another." I prayed and the chill eased off. Once I ran to pray as soon as the chill started and the ague stopped almost immediately. I had to keep heating the kettle for the water bags. He was so terribly yellow, even his eyeballs. Oh, how long the day seemed, and I watched for Brother Stewart!

"Sails" in the afternoon. At last help was coming! Norman longed to see Brother Stewart, but still would not let me send. But oh, that boat came so slowly and at dark it was not in yet. Another night alone, but not for one minute would I harbor any thought but that Norman would get better, and he always believed he would get better. I assured him I was praying for him. No matter how I felt, I would not go to him but with a smiling face. He said he had prayed and he knew that Jesus loved him when I asked him. "I have prayed," he said several times, when I told him to pray. He even feared for me to sponge him because of the awful chills. He would get out of bed as he had no bedpan and it was so hard to urinate—he was getting terribly weak—it was an effort even to lift a hand. At 8:00 I sponged him and went to bed. I was up most of the night, with snatches of sleep between.

He longed for me to stay with him, but kept urging me to rest. "If we both went down, and no one to look after us, what would we do?" I had to keep the primus going, for I could not leave him long enough to light the stove.

Tuesday, May 4

When I was up before daylight he began to seem delirious and gradually grew worse all day. As I looked out in the moonlight I could see the ship had anchored. Oh, at last help was near! At daylight I would send to him and he would go to Atchin for me. But daylight came and not a native was near. I strained my eyes and ears for the first sign of a native, but hour after hour passed with no one to send to the boat. Help so near and yet so far! All the day before I had begged coconuts as that seemed the only thing Norman could keep down at all, and they had promised to be down early. Finally, at nine o'clock, I heard the pig call, and later along came some natives. I sent a letter to the captain, and he came up. I showed him Norman and then begged him to take a letter for me. He said he could not, as one of his boat's crew was inland. Finally he said he would send a boat, then he left. The natives hung around for a while, but finally they too left and I was alone again. I watched for that boat to round the point, but it did not go.

After dinner I could wait no longer, so I called to the voices in the gully. Again and again I called, and they answered and laughed, but would not come near, although they said Norman would not live. Oh, those hours seemed like weeks. At last, at two o'clock, they came. I begged with tear-filled eyes for someone to do something, telling them I feared he would not live through the night. They saw him, and knew it all, but only laughed at my pleadings. I tried to send another letter to the captain, but they went a little way and returned with a made-up message. I begged them to take our boat and oars, and when a boat went around the point I thought they had gone. But they returned, saying there were no rowlocks. The captain came up, this time agreeing to send one of his boats and a man, if I could get a boat crew. Again I did all that pleading and appealing could do.

Oh, if they only knew how precious those moments were to me, and how I longed to be permitted to stay at the side of my darling, they would not have kept me from him! A sound, and I would rush to see if those fevered lips had a word for me, and then as he would again swoon, the sight that was tearing out my heart would send me back to beg them for help.

The captain left, and at last the boys agreed to go if they could find the

rowlocks. But at dusk they came back saying it was too late to go. Oh, must I spend another night without any hope of help? That seemed almost the last straw. But they buoyed me up with the promise that at daylight they would be down and go, and in the meantime Vilvil promised faithfully to look up a crew.

Only a few words had come from those precious lips that day but a kiss whenever I had asked for it. Oh, if I could only have stayed right with him, perhaps I should have had more. "I do love you, Norman," "I love you, too, darling." Again, "I fear I am going to lose my dear boy." A surprised look, and he shook his head. I knew he was ready to go; why should I torture him with the thought? So I said, "No, you are not going to leave me, are you? You are going to get better." Once his expression changed and he nodded. Earlier in the day I said, "I am so sorry I have been cross with you, Norman." "You haven't been cross with me, darling." "Oh yes, I have sometimes. You will forgive me, won't you?" "Yes, and you will forgive me, too." Again I asked if he would like me to pray for him, and he said Yes, so I prayed aloud. Ten minutes later he said, "I am thinking, I am thinking." "Yes, what are you thinking about?" "I am thinking about that prayer." At six o'clock, when I asked if he knew I was there, "Yes," but when I asked if he could see me, he said, "No."

At my request for company, Bukul, a cripple covered with sores, was selected to stay with me. I had asked for a man and his wife, but a questioning smile and a few remarks made me know that I should say no more, for I must let them think they had my perfect confidence. However, sometimes during the long night which followed, the thoughts of my helpless condition, if that man cared to take advantage, crossed my mind. But through it all I had to be continually thankful, for considering the sudden cessation of [my] fever, and the strength despite the lack of food and sleep. Now I was free to sit by the side of my boy, but no longer did words come from his lips. He had no chills, and his fever had kept down all day. I prayed as I had never prayed before. "We let go of the arm of the Lord too soon," came to my mind. But now, whenever I felt to plead for his life, that I had prayed for a turn, my prayer had not been answered. I must be resigned, so with each prayer my Father helped me add, "Thy will be done." Still pled that if it must come, it might not come through the long, dark hours of the night, and this prayer was answered.

Norman recognized me by a look (although from glassy eyes) or a groan, and gave me a kiss whenever he seemed to rouse, and I asked for it until about ten o'clock. At eleven o'clock I gave him half an hour to live. His

temperature was still 101 degrees F., but his pulse varied from 120 to 160 beats per minute. I made Bukul stay right in the room with me, for I felt I could not bear to be alone. Still I felt that sustaining Hand right through it all, and never for a minute did I question whether it was right. This surely would touch those hard hearts, and if so, hard as it was, I was willing to have it so. As hard as they were I could say with Christ, "Father, forgive them, for they know not what they do," for we both loved him. I talked to that man as I had never talked to anyone before, telling him how we had prayed for them, and how sad we had felt at their lack of response. I tried to show him it was all for them. I felt no feelings of bitterness toward them, only sorrow that they knew no better.

Wednesday, May 5

At one o'clock the breathing became better and the pulse not so violent. Slowly Norman brightened up a bit. Bukul, too, saw an improvement, but still I knew this was often the case just before the last, so quieted my hopes. Then Bukul said, "Suppose he black man he savvy live back again," and suggested I give him milk and water. I tried it and Norman formed his lips to receive it from the spoon, and even raised his hand to wipe his mouth when some ran down. I began to build up hopes. Bukul went to sleep in the kitchen. Surely the crisis was past and I was to have my dear boy back again. He even tried to respond and kiss me again when I called his name. All that night I had pled that as I could not send a message, Brother Stewart might be awakened out of his sleep with the strong impression that we needed him, and now even if my Norman must go perhaps he would remain till Brother Stewart would come and see him. We had so longed for Brother Stewart to come. "Do you see the launch? I wish Brother Stewart would come." So he kept me always watching.

Again we tried to raise the boys who were sleeping just across the gully, even giving the signal we were to give if the end really came, but they only responded that we wait till morning, followed by laughter. I picked up some crochet work to try to calm my mingled feelings—half joyous with hope and yet trying not to allow my hopes to rise too high lest they should be all crushed again. Surely my Father would not give me such a promise if there were not some meaning to it, and yet it might only be the answer to my prayer that the end should not come in the night. It was hope constantly being repulsed and yet trying to fight back fear. Which should win?

Hard as it all was, my Father strengthened my faith, so that I never once doubted, nor was my confidence in Him shaken. I knew it all must be for the

best somehow. Again and again I pled that if it could be to His honor and glory, my darling might be spared me, but He gave me strength to add, "Thy will be done." Perhaps my Father saw that the tests that would come to my dear Norman might be more than his faith would be able to stand, and so was placing him in safe keeping for me. Perhaps too it was the only way our prayers for those people whom we both loved, and for whom we had worked so hard, might be realized. If it would lead them to my Saviour, was I willing to make the sacrifice? Yes, I believe that with all my heart I would answer "Yes," for would Norman not be willing if he could realize it? I believe he would. But again the prayer was on my lips, "If it can be Thy will, Oh my Father, save him, but Thy will be done. And if he must go, give me strength to bear it, and Oh for his sake, keep me faithful that I may have him back again."

At 5:00 a.m. I could see he was failing again. But I had wept till I had no more tears to shed. With the first signs of dawn I began to watch for that promised boat's crew, for at last Bukul remembered seeing Norman hide the rowlocks under a stone. Again I roused the boys and had them whistle across the gully, but this time there was no response. Perhaps they were on their way across to us. But an hour slowly passed and we began to hear the pig calls in the surrounding gullies and hills. Norman was now having no more chills, and for this I was thankful, for his suffering was terrible. I had prayed when the last one came that he might have no more, and then the thought flashed across my mind, "Perhaps your prayers may be answered in a way you don't want." As soon as it was light enough I kept rushing to the verandah and straining my eyes—first up to see if I could distinguish a figure coming over the brows, and then to the ocean to search for a boat coming ashore—but all in vain.

It seemed more than I could endure, and I paced the floor in agony. Hungry? A sense of duty made me chew a bit of zwieback. Once again I turned to Bukul, pleading that he go to the beach and try to signal the captain, but he said it was no use. Then to add to my anguish, he told me to go, saying he would look after Norman. But no, I would never leave him with breath remaining.

All this time my poor boy lay, the only sign of life being those heavy breaths and terrible fast heart-beats and gurgling. Finally, at almost nine o'clock, there was a murmur of voices, but as they got nearer there was a silence, and a few minutes later they were in the distance below me. They had slipped around another track through the bush and dodged me. Bukul had left a while before ostensibly to go to the beach, but really to feed his pigs. I had begged for some woman to come down, but I had not seen one. Again

there was a murmur of voices and at last Vilvil and several men appeared. What a relief! But it was only momentary. He had come to say he had no boat's crew. Again I showed him my dying boy and he really seemed to be touched, and said he would send someone and hurried off to the beach.

As the morning wore on and it drew nearer the time when Brother Stewart usually came, I watched more closely—but all in vain. Oh, how I longed for someone, only if it were an unsympathetic native! And I prayed that if my boy was taken I might not be alone. Minutes seemed like hours as I sat there with my hand under that chin; and now and then placing a kiss on that brow—for all the kisses he ever received must be while there was still life, and longing for someone. Finally, about 11:30 a.m., along came Kambi with a company of men, and a few minutes later, Vilvil with some more men and the news that someone was rounding the point. Could it be Brother Stewart? No, it was only a canoe. Still it might mean help.

Kambi with a towel kept chasing the flies away. The natives had gathered in, and we watched those fleeting breaths. Those eyes that had looked so lovingly upon me would never do so again. Those lips that had so often formed kisses and spoken loving words, would do so no more. Those hands that had so often been thrown around me, or worked for my comfort were still. Oh how I longed for just one more word, just one more caress! Then about ten o'clock came those last two long expirations. His eyes flew open, and I knew he was gone. It was only then that the last vestige of hope was really gone, for while there is life there is hope. "Alone!" Oh how few know the meaning of that word. If there was only someone to stand by me and bear with me the terrible anguish of that hour! Until then the world could laugh, and the world could frown, but what cared I once I had talked it over with him. Now it seemed that my wall of protection was torn from me.

It was not fear of the natives that harassed me. I knew my danger, but felt no fear on their account. It was the terrible thought of facing life's battles alone that shook my whole frame as I closed those eyes and threw my head on my arm beside him. But only for a moment could I linger thus. If only someone else were there to just take charge of things I could leave him now; but no, there was no one, so my hands must perform those last rites. As if touched by an electric current, I sprang into action. The natives helped me lift him onto a board and remove the bedding. And for this they wanted pay. But it had rather been a privilege which I was loathe to allow, that they should touch my dead with their rough hands.

Then I turned the natives out. A new shirt formed a shroud. After all, it

was a blessing that I had to get up and do something. Even at that moment I had much to be thankful for, not the least was the presence of mind that had been given me all through. Then too, when Norman went down, I myself had no fever. I covered him with a sheet and placed a towel over his face under the net.

Just as I finished laying Norman out, the Tonmiel boys arrived, Natan, Leli Sal or Natan Soluperi and Jugleli. They seemed like a godsend, and I never appreciated the arrival of anyone more. I believe they were especially sent in answer to my prayer. Watch the tears roll down those brown cheeks as they gaze upon the face of one who had been their teacher, then try to convince anyone that natives do not feel. Hastily I snatched up the letter I had written bit by bit and placed it in an envelope without even taking time to add that the end had really come. This I placed in their hands, begging that they let nothing detain them, that they stop neither for food or rest until they had delivered the letter to Atchin. When after anxious watching I saw the canoe round the point, I felt that at last help was near.

All that afternoon and many times during the night, I pictured them nearing Atchin at last, so early the next morning I imagined Brother Stewart receiving the letter and flying to my help. Our hearts' desire and Norman's constant wish, that he should again see and talk with Brother Stewart, was not to be realized. But now, I thought that some other eyes would at least look upon him anyway for that letter had gone. Oh, if Brother Stewart might see him before he should be laid to rest! I left his tie for Brother Stewart to tie, and worried not about where he should be laid to rest, in full confidence that Brother Stewart would be there and take the whole responsibility.

Now my thoughts turned to myself. I must do the work of two now. So I must do all in my power to keep calm and keep my strength up. I had chewed a bit of zwieback for my breakfast, and now from a sense of duty I went across to the kitchen and had a meal. What wouldn't I give to have that meal interrupted by my boy, but no, I must eat alone. The second tomato from our lovely patch, with some tinned apricots, zwieback, and biscuits formed my lunch. But first I had taken a walk across the yard and down over the back fence to gaze again at the beautiful view across the gully. A scrap of paper with a picture of a mother holding in her hands a baby brought home more forcibly the realization that that hope, the anticipation of which had given me many a happy thought, should never be mine. I was just beginning to know what it all meant. Still, through it all, my confidence in my God was not shaken, and never did I question "Why?"

The hope of the resurrection and a soon-coming Saviour never seemed so dear, but how could I wait till that time should come? So I went back to the room and knelt in prayer by the bedside of that loved one. I could thank my Father that he was safe—kept for me. If this could result in souls I was willing to make the sacrifice, and I know he would have been, for we really did love these people. If they would only allow me to stay on and work for them! As I walked around the garden in which we had been working just the week before and gazed upon those gullies and hills, I felt I couldn't leave that lovely little home with those people I had learned to love. No, I would work on alone. But I knew that could not be, and as it all came home that I must leave it all, it seemed to double my sorrow.

These and many other thoughts filled my mind as my hands were busy; for there was a big wash to do, and the house had not been cleaned while Norman was so ill. A little later the native captain came up, and as I took him in and turned back the sheet the tears streamed down the brown cheeks. All afternoon he and the natives sat around, and he offered to make a coffin out of the new timber we had for our table and safe. I was tired, but how thankful I was that my time was fully occupied. At last nightfall came and the natives started to go home. I had urged Vilvil not to leave me alone, but to send a man and his wife to keep me company. This he promised to do, but I feared he would fail (as he did). At last [he] persuaded an old man and Atri to stay with me. Later the captain himself and one boy returned, as the boy alone would not come. I took my chair out and we all slept on the verandah. Slept! Yes, part of the time, and when it was impossible to sleep I aroused the boys and talked to them, for I felt I could not bear to be alone with my thoughts. Somehow those thoughts haunted me and I dreaded them. All that night and the next day I would catch myself listening for a call or a stir, and again the awful realization returned, "I will never be called again."

Thursday, May 6

At last daybreak came. I watched that shadowy coast take shape, and strained my eyes for the first glimpse of the launch. Surely my trial is sufficient, I thought, and the Lord will not give me the severe test of laying my loved one to rest alone.

At daylight the captain and his boy left me, promising to return later and fix up a coffin if Brother Stewart did not arrive. Hour after hour I waited, the suspense growing unbearable. Oh, if someone would only come, even if only a native to sit on the verandah! Someone I could speak to. Finally,

about 9:00 a.m., pig calls began to resound in the distance and come nearer. How welcome even those sounds were, and then I began to hear voices. But again the voices died away just as I expected someone to come out from the trees. Then a few minutes later, as if to mock me, I heard the voices echoing up from the valley below. They had quietly slipped past.

Finally, at two o'clock, I could bear it no longer. Having a long last look at that precious dust, I locked the house and made my way to the beach. There I learned that the captain had been to Matanavat and found that the letter had not been hurried on as I had requested. Quite likely Brother Stewart was still quite ignorant of our need. I pled for the captain to do something or send someone, but they only laughed in my face. Once more I wended my way back up that hill. How terrible it seemed to be climbing that hill alone; we had always gone together.

Once more my eyes found their tears, and I wept aloud as I hurried up the hill. Somehow I felt I had done a terrible thing to leave Norman even that long. I could hardly wait till I reached the house to rush into the bedroom and see that everything was all right. Then I came out and threw myself on the bed and poured out my grief aloud. "Oh Father, must I bear it all alone? Can You not send someone?" I was ready to say I could bear it alone, but the words died on my lips. No, if I hadn't a faith that could sustain me through trial it wasn't worth much. But how I longed for the touch of some loving hand or the sound of a voice to break the terrible silence. While Norman was still living, there was something to keep up for, but now the tension was relaxed. Only the work we both loved still buoyed me up. Yet, through it all I felt the close presence of my Saviour.

At length I heard voices. The captain came up on the verandah and spoke. Together we walked up the hill and across the flat to search for a suitable place to lay that precious dust. He wished it to be close to the house, but we finally chose a secluded spot some yards from the house, under the shade of two hardwood trees. Bamboos on the other side closed in the sacred area. Several times the captain and natives wanted to lay him away, but I kept putting them off, still feeling Brother Stewart might be impressed to come. I felt I could not lay him to rest without Brother Stewart seeing him once more, for he had so longed for Brother Stewart to come. As the shadows lengthened, I realized we could wait no longer. The grave had been dug, but when I went to see it, it was so shallow I could not rest, so begged them to dig it deeper. The thought of wild pigs and native customs were too vivid in my mind to let him rest so near the surface.

I felt I had stood all I could, so now gave the captain and one of his

crew a sheet, a towel, and two native mats. One mat was wrapped and tied around him, while the other formed an outer covering. While they did this, I went out once more and looked at our little garden. Then I took one last look at Norman, and it was more than I could stand. It was better for me to leave him to them now. Several times that captain asked if I was ready, but each time I would scan the coast longingly for the sign of a launch, and wave them back.

Now the sun was creeping lower, so I must give the word. They bore that precious body around the side of the hill while I followed. As we reached the spot, that hole still looked shallow, so all waited while I urged them to dig still deeper. At last we laid him carefully in, facing the hill over which those lived for whom he so willingly gave his life. All through his illness, never once had a murmur or regret escaped his lips. When a service was mentioned, the captain said, "We savvy make him church along Master." My heart was too full for words, so I just stood silently while he repeated a service he had learned and then offered a prayer in his own language. I could not understand anything. I wished they would let me get out of sight and hearing before they did any more. So I stuck my fingers in my ears and ran as fast as I could.

As I gazed out over the ocean, the sun had already dipped into the sea—a symbol, it seemed, of the end of my joy and happiness. I felt a determination to meet life's battles bravely. Because sorrow had crossed my life was no reason why I should cast a shadow over everyone I would meet. How selfish to seek comfort by reminding others of my grief. Before I saw a white face I determined that I would, with my Saviour's help, show a bright face to the world. My sorrow would be sealed in my own heart, my tears shed in the dark alone. We had always realized our danger from natives, and while we never said much, each knew the feelings which might sometime be ours. Once Norman asked me where, if anything happened, I would like to rest. He said he would rather be at Atchin. I said I would rather rest among the people for whom we were living. That was all, but now I felt that even if I could have chosen, I would rather have that precious mound bearing witness just where he fell. We had never thought of sickness separating us, just the natives.

I wrote a few lines to Brother Stewart, not knowing how he would get it. The local natives had become tired and gone home, with only the captain, three of his boat's crew, and I at the grave. The captain and his men returned. Wednesday morning I learned that the natives had stolen some of our fowls, and I began to realize that it was not right for me to stay here

alone even if I could. Should they know that I was alone, it might place temptation in their way. Not that I feared, for there had been a wonderful sense of a keeping and sustaining Power. But I just must have someone to talk to; the thing I dreaded most was to be left alone with my thoughts. Upon my request the captain promised me company, but said they must all return to the ship first.

I knew what that promise meant, so made him leave his boys while he returned. They were too afraid to even eat. Two boys stayed through the night. I dragged my couch out onto the verandah and stayed there, wrapped in my rug. I would not ask them inside to sleep, so we all slept on the verandah together. Once again, whenever I could not sleep, I would wake them up and make them talk with me.

Friday, May 7

At daylight, while the captain was anxious to be with his ship, he promised to see that I had company at nights until Brother Stewart should come. I now concluded that he had never received any messages from me, and that I would simply have to wait till his expected trip the coming week. I had not been alone very long when dear old Nikambat arrived. He had broken their rules of mourning and hurried down to see the face of him whom he called master and really loved. He did not say much, but that firm handclasp and those few words of affection for the master showed a warm heart under a brown skin. He was anxious to know if I would stay and teach, and at first did not like the idea of a new master he did not know. We had a long talk. I felt that dear old man was, in his own way, doing all he knew. He still had just as keen an interest in school, and promised to be friendly to whoever might be sent to take our place. He wished me to keep the money he had given Norman. All morning he sat around ordering his men to do little things I asked.

About 9:00 a.m. the captain returned, so I asked him if he would take me to Atchin. This he reluctantly agreed to, saying he would leave at noon. He caught the remaining fowls and put them in a box, and I packed a few necessary clothes in my suitcase, and a coat, a rug, two bottles of water, and a few other necessary things. Oh how hard it was to bid farewell to that little home. Once more I looked around the garden and ran over the edge of the hill to take a last look into the gully. Last of all, I went around the hill to gaze for the first time on that fresh mound of earth. I felt I could even stand that if only I could stay and work for those people. But to think that I must go and leave it all—my grief was too deep for tears. That last

six months had been the happiest of our lives.

At 1:00 p.m. we started. The captain had tried to get something for me to eat, and I was able to eat some crackers and jam. The wind was good, and we reached the Tonmiel landing before dark. I was anxious to go to the village to see if anyone had gone to Atchin. It was raining, and the road was somewhat changed, so I was not sure of the way when we neared the village. We met some of the people among others, Billi, and found the letters had been sent to the next village. It was nearly dark, so after a promise of old friends to bring me some bananas and other fruit, we hurried back to the beach. It was now dark, so the captain was anxious to return to the boat, and signaled his crew. They all rowed off, leaving me sitting on a canoe in the rain expecting each minute to hear voices from the village. Minutes, hours passed as I sat there in the rain, cold, wet, and alone. No one came. Finally about 9:00 pm., there was a splash of oars, and the boat's crew came to tell me that as the wind was favorable, their master had decided to leave for Santo (40 miles north) and that I might go with him, as he feared the sea to take me on to Atchin. Not knowing what else to do, I scrambled into the boat and we were soon alongside the ship.

As I heard the captain's proposition I felt I could not accept it. He would not even promise to take me to friends on Santo, although this was only a short distance from his destination. I was sure Pastor Stewart had never received any message from me, although at Espiegel Bay we left a note with a Frenchman anchored there; and should I get to Santo there would be no way of getting back or sending him word. I felt wholly unprepared for such a trip, so asked to be rowed around to Matanavat, some eight miles away. There I would at least be on Malekulan soil, and could walk if no other way opened. He finally consented, but instructed his crew to land me on the beach and to do no more. It was dark and they were less acquainted with the coast than I, so we had quite a time finding the passage. About 10:00 p.m. we at last found our way through the passage in the rocks and I was landed with my things on the sand. As they had a lantern, I constrained them to go with me to our old school drum that used to sound out the hour for school. We beat it, hoping that someone from the village would come down.

Then we hurried back to the sand. In a few minutes the light was fading from view, the splash of the oars grew fainter, and that word *alone* came back to me with still more force. No boat light lingered in the distance. Now the only sounds were waves splashing on the shore.

Even that was acceptable company, also the patter of gentle rain, and

> now and then the weird screech of a night bird. There must be something to break the silence, so I sang aloud and repeated texts of Scripture. The promises of Psalm 91 came to me. As time passed and no one came, the only thing left to do was wait till the moon came up and then make my way toward the village. About 11:00 p.m. the moon should begin to show; God's clocks never disappoint us. But the moon could only help for a few yards, and then I just feel my way along a narrow path through the pitch darkness of the jungle. [Regretfully, the rest of Alma's diary was lost. She told me personally about the rest of the journey.]

When the rain stopped, the moon peeked through the clouds, allowing her to see a path, which she followed to a village. When a native appeared, she made known her plight. This village was Matanavat, Norman and Alma's first residence on Malekula, and therefore not unknown to her. The native took her to an empty house, spread some fresh leaves on the ground, and told her to rest in peace, for he would protect her. Being exhausted, she slept until morning. This day being Sabbath, she spent it resting in this village. The next day she felt able to go on. The natives escorted her several miles toward the next village, then sent her on alone, explaining that this was not their territory and it was unsafe for them to go farther. Men with muskets guarded the tribal boundaries. So she walked to the next village alone, carrying her suitcase and a cushion. The people, who were friendly enough, directed her to the next village east. From village to village she trudged some sixteen miles till she saw the sea on the eastern side of the island.

Atchin at last! And just a quarter of a mile across the water were the Stewarts, the companionship, support, and sympathy for which she had prayed. She put down her bundle, sat down on the shore, and looked across to her earthly haven of rest and consolation. Now she must somehow bridge the distance between Atchin and Malekula. Being short of faith to try walking on water, she waited. It was useless to call across the waters with no one in sight, so she looked around for someone to canoe her across.

At last several natives came sauntering along the coastal path carrying a canoe. They were obviously surprised to see a white woman sitting alone. She appealed to them to take her to Atchin in their canoe, and they agreed. A few deft strokes and they shot toward the other shore, where Alma anxiously stepped out. She followed the familiar path to the mission house, knocked at the door, and collapsed in the arms of Mrs. Stewart. No message, she learned, had ever reached the Stewarts.

ALMA'S DEPARTURE FOR SYDNEY

Norman Wiles died May 5, 1920. Forty days and forty nights later, Pastor Stewart wrote in touching terms of their great loss of a dear friend and coworker:

> Today is a sad day for us here, as we are just getting ready to take Sister Wiles to Bushman's Bay, about twenty miles down the coast to meet the steamer, on her return to Sydney. With her departure we shall more fully sense our loss. While she has been with us it has been a mutual comfort, but now we shall be left alone. The empty mission house at Big Nambus makes us feel sad. While Brother and Sister Wiles were there a torch kept burning in that dark place. But now that they are gone the burden seems to press upon us continually. Surely there are others who will come and pick up the fallen standard.

Alma was distressed about leaving the work on Malekula. She begged to remain, but the brethren thought it unwise. Nor did they think it advisable for her to return to service to this place of tragedy. She returned to America, where she completed her nurse's training, then spent many years in service in New Guinea, and later Ile Ife, Nigeria. Norman's grave was cemented by Pastor Stewart and surrounded by a picket fence. Then he placed at the head a polished stone in which he had graven:

NORMAN WILES
MISSIONARY
Born August 25, 1892 Died May 5, 1920
"Greater love hath no man than this"

CHAPTER 10

REPLACEMENT FOR NORMAN WILES

In 1922, at a session of the Australian Union Conference, Harold Blunden, secretary of Island Missions, gave his report:

> Forty-six years have rolled by since the angel of Revelation 14 began his flight across the waters of the Pacific to the many islands resting upon its bosom. Thirty-six years ago our first converts embraced the truths on the romantic island of Pitcairn. From that time to the present our work has gradually extended, gathering strength in expansion until today we have an army of 66 white workers and 59 natives heralding the Third Angel's Message to the many nations, kindreds, tongues and peoples who dwell in our most interesting mission field; while 1,131 baptized members, together with over 2,500 other adherents, rejoice in a knowledge of this message. Two printing plants are issuing literature in five languages.

Blunden expanded on the vastness of the field and the responsibility of the church to provide men and the means to meet the gospel challenge of thousands of islands. He told of his visit to the New Hebrides.

> On one of these journeys we made our way to the Big Nambus territory, the scene of the labors of our late Brother Wiles. While there we witnessed the treachery of these semi-nude savages in the shooting of a boat's crew within two hundred yards of where we stood. We were made to appreciate

the dangers which lurked ever near the little home on the hillside where dwelt our brave missionary and courageous wife. Today that lonely grave on those foothills below the village of Nikambet makes a mute appeal to us to take up once more the work which our brother launched for that cannibal people. Over two years have flown by since this enterprise was so suddenly brought to an end, and still no response has been made to the appeal of that lonely grave.

The Big Nambus people are still waiting. Surely at this conference some brave hand will grasp the standard let drop by our fallen comrade, and carry it to victory amidst the wild tribes of the hills of cannibal Malekula.

To find a couple of the caliber of Norman and Alma Wiles was no simple assignment. They must be young enough, mature enough, and tried enough; willing enough, selfless enough and brave enough; dedicated enough, kind enough, firm enough, knowledgeable enough, and wise enough. They must be submissive and aggressive, practical and hopeful, consumed with the commission to go into the world with the gospel; prepared to sacrifice homeland comforts and live among a crude and primitive people. Who would qualify, and who would respond? The lot finally fell on Will and Louisa Smith with their six-year-old son, Ivan.

Not from the ranks of frontline evangelists with powerful platform appeal did Will come, nor from the academic area with impressive letters enhancing his name. Neither was he of the keen, calculating kind, nor of the philosopher type, formulating ideas for people to ponder. Will Smith was a devoted, self-effacing servant who knew his Lord personally and lived His Word. The same could be said of Lou, as we endearingly called her (she was my older sister). Together they spent seven years on Malekula.

Smith had come from a Roman Catholic family in New Zealand. At eleven years of age he served as altar boy in his church. His mother passed away about that time. Her last wish was that he become a priest. Though he set his sights on this achievement, the family went into the hotel business, with stables, racehorses, and coaching contracts, so that Will became an experienced driver—enjoying his work. But his health was poor. An Adventist book salesman came one day and sold him *Man the Masterpiece.* Reading this, he learned of the Adventist sanitarium in Christchurch, New Zealand, so he went there in search of robust health. He not only regained his health, but in the congenial atmosphere of the institution found a new philosophy for living. My uncle, Arthur Brandstater, manager of this institution, awakened in Will an interest in basic Bible truth. Here, too, he met my sister, where she worked as a nurse. Then he learned of Longburn Adventist College and applied to be accepted there as a student, though still a

Roman Catholic. Here he pursued his Bible studies and studied other subjects, then went on to ministerial training, now determined to preach Christ and the everlasting gospel. His conversion was compete and definite. He was baptized as his Master had been, and at about the same age. He finished his course, pledged his life in service, and was appointed to the ministry in North New Zealand. Then he married Louisa Brandstater, who attended the same college.

The characters of the Wileses and the Smiths were remarkably similar. Both Norman and Alma were singularly devout and dedicated, as were Will and Lou. Norman experienced an unusually definite conversion, as did Will. Alma was of the particularly warm and pious kind, as Lou had been in our home. As a young lady she kept us younger ones in the "straight and narrow way."

The Smiths did not go to Malekula right away. It was necessary to approach the work there again with care, even though the Big Nambus still called for a teacher. The newcomers were to be initiated into mission life by working at Atchin for a time before locating on Malekula.

TRAGEDY NARROWLY AVERTED

Not long after Will's arrival on Atchin, he faced a potentially dangerous situation. "Ordinarily upon the Sabbath morning," he wrote, "both Brother Parker and I make evangelical visits among the heathen in their different villages. Today, however, Brother Parker went as usual, but I remained at the mission house, having had the fever the day before. Soon after Brother Parker had left, we were startled when one of our mission boys ran to our door and shouted, 'Somebody's trying to shoot the people.' We could see by the expression on his face that something unusual was happening."

> Sure enough, it was discovered that some labor recruiters had brought eight muskets and a revolver ashore. Their guns were loaded for their deadly work if necessary. Mrs. Smith and I called upon our heavenly Father for wisdom, then ran down to the shore and found seventy or eighty natives in an awful frenzy. It seemed as if everyone was shouting at once. Different ones had muskets in their hands, and we were surprised that no one had been shot before we arrived. I ran to the spot where the people were gathered and tried to pacify them.
>
> The white man, the master of the ship, had attempted to shoot one of the Atchin native boys. I asked him to unload his revolver. He did so and gave me the chamber, which was fully loaded. In the meantime, Mrs. Smith had been trying to pacify the natives ashore who had been

provoked to fight the natives from the ship.

I could see that the only way to prevent disaster was to separate the Atchin people from these men. The Lord helped us to silence them, and to get them to agree to cease fighting and shouting. The white man had already promised to go, and the natives calmed down when I told them this. The trouble originated when our natives objected to the tactics of the natives seeking to recruit the Atchinese. They tried to allure the Atchinese women onto the boat. Malresre was the first one to raise an objection, so they sought to get him to fight. He refused, saying he was a Christian. His example served as a leaven to bring peace. The natives told us afterwards that if we had not come to their help something serious would have occurred. We united in thankfulness to God that no one was killed.

About this time missionary Parker reported,

Last week a Vao* man brought his baby boy five weeks old and gave him to the mission. At first he wanted us to look after him until he was a big boy, then he, the father, would pay money and take him back again. We told him that we would accept him only if the father would give the baby entirely into our hands and renounce any claim as a father on him. This he did, signing a paper to this effect, so now we have added a member to our family.

This is a strange experience, as these people usually will not give up their boys. A girl, maybe, but a boy, never! Many Atchinese could not believe it. They have crowded around to see the baby. Sister Smith is acting as mother, and Sister Parker as grandmother. When little Samuel, for that is now his name, came to us he was skin and bones. His mother had died when he was just twenty-six days old. Other women with children would nurse him, but they soon got tired of that and refused to nourish him any longer. He had been without food for some time when he was brought to us, and his voice was a mere peep.

We have had him now just five days, and flesh is coming back on his bones. He has gained half a pound. Our boys here say he is to be a missionary to Vao when he grows up. We have dedicated him to the Lord as Hannah did her little Samuel.

* * * * *

---

* Vao is an island just north of Atchin.

Samuel grew up under the care of the Smiths on Malekula, was educated at the Adventist mission school, and became a missionary to several islands of the New Hebrides. He has been an ordained minister of Malekula for many years and is highly esteemed in the New Hebrides. In April 1979, he was sent as a delegate to the General Conference session held in Dallas, Texas.

CHAPTER 11

HEATHEN HUNGER FOR A BETTER WAY

The missionary did not always have to hard sell his Christian faith to the people of Malekula. Christianity, with its faith, hope, and freedom from fear, was clearly appealing to the natives. Don Nicholson, missionary on the island of Ambrym, who visited Malekula for a year during the absence of a resident missionary, tells the way it was at the time of the Parkers' return and the Smiths' coming to the New Hebrides:

> For the past twelve months the villages along the coast of west Malekula have been throbbing with impulses of a new order. It could hardly be called an interest; but there was a hope, a spirit of inquiry, men and women groping in the dark for something better than their surroundings. These villages are in a deplorable condition, and if a change does not come it will soon be too late to save them. Infanticide and intertribal fighting, as well as recruiting, have reduced the villages to impotency.
>
> News soon travels, and natives are quick to notice any change. When the people on Atchin and Ambrym made decisions for the Gospel, people whom we had never met before began to come down to the passages along the coast and send messages asking us to visit them. At first they were elated when Tonmiel built a new village of a different type, but soon they learned that the station was a challenge to paganism, for now they would not attend feasts or dances. The old men saw in this attitude the destruction of their system, and their own death, for any departure from

the rules of taboo restrictions is supposed to allow the evil spirits to work their will upon men.

Nicholson told how from Matanavat the Tonmiel people learned the gospel and took it to their old enemies at Espiegle Bay, who had murdered many of the Tonmiel tribe. Now as Christians the Tonmiel people would not fight, but instead showed their former enemies the better way of life and won them to Christ. The missionary continues:

> The Espiegle chief made a request to see me, so one day I took some Tonmiel boys and went down to their passage. We drew near to the sandy beach in the dinghy, expecting to meet our friends, but suddenly our crew "back watered" and exclaimed: "These are man bushy." These bushmen were notorious, unpredictable, and dangerous, so there was a moment of panic. However, the boys soon learned that this company of about fifty bushmen were friendly, and we landed. The chief laid his musket against a tree, and we conversed about a mission. After half an hour of friendly talk we presented our conditions: separation from the village life and all obligations to paganism, and a guarantee of protection for the teacher.
>
> These people, and the tribes surrounding them, have committed cold-blooded murders on both white men and natives. Their passages are considered so dangerous that recruiters will not land there. The chief admitted that this all was true, but said great injustices had been committed against them. He pointed out that his own son was detained on a plantation against his will, and could not return to be chief, succeeding his father. However, he guaranteed that no more shooting would take place here if we would give them a mission. A piece of ground was selected for the mission site, and we left feeling assured.
>
> Down below Espiegle Bay was another passage through the rugged shoreline, Malua Bay, where the Big Nambus come for trade. When these people learned of the prospects of an Espiegle Bay mission, they wanted to leave their heathen village, build a new one, and accept a teacher. This was the place where the chief's brother was shot by a punitive expedition, and the chief vowed not to eat till he had eaten a white man. Norman Wiles was stalked for several days. So we were extra cautious in meeting them and received their deputation on the vessel. However they seemed quite friendly, and are making overtures for a mission.
>
> After three years' absence, C. H. Parker again visited the Big Nambus. On reaching the Espiegle Bay people's town we found that the chief had

been returned by the government. He had been indentured by a Frenchman on Epi for one year, but at the expiration of the time they would not let him go. The time ran on to two and a half years. His people pled with us to approach the government for his release. I wrote to Mr. King, the British Commissioner, who took the matter up with the French government, stating that he wanted the matter attended to at once. This resulted in his return to his people. The French told the chief I had written to the British that he should be released. We had an animated conversation, and a good service with them. They were very responsive.

My heart was cheered by the reception that the Big Nambus chief and his people gave us. They were talkative, and we were able to get close to them. It seemed like the time when I first gained their confidence back in 1915. As a final touch, the chief sent for my old friend Nikambat. He would not do this before; he always put me off.

What a meeting that was! Dear old man, what a look of love he gave me! Then we embraced. He was like a child. It was hard to leave him. Malun Vauvau and Nikambat each brought us big yams. This showed real friendship and love. These yams, four to six feet long, are especially planted for worship of their ancestors. They are not common yams. These men seemed very anxious to make our visits frequent. Once we get this work started again we will have our hands more than full.

About twelve months after coming to the New Hebrides, the Smiths took up residence in Wileses' former territory on Malekula. The native teacher from Ambrym did an admirable job in sustaining and developing the interest at Tonmiel, which was an extension of the Matanavat effort. The coastal villages were calling for a mission. In May 1924, the Smiths were asked to take over the work on Malekula and make that their home. Pastor C. H. Parker took them by launch from Atchin Island on the eastern side, around to the western side of Malekula, past Espiegle Bay to the village of Tonmiel. This was the most responsive and stable mission interest on Malekula, a point from which the missionary could survey the land and determine where best to locate a permanent mission headquarters. Smith wrote,

We are now at Tonmiel, Malekula, where for about twenty months we have had a native teacher. When one remembers that Malekula has been a place of murder and cannibalism, one feels that nothing but the power of God can bring about such a transformation. We are glad to know that the Gospel has lost none of its power, and we look forward to great things. The Tonmiel

> people seem to desire the things of God. When we came, almost all the men and women were smoking tobacco. Yesterday one of the leaders told me that the women and most of the men had broken up their pipes.
>
> We have been settled in our native house about three weeks. We are living right among the natives who have moved in from their native settlement and made a fresh village. Many of the people give definite evidence that they have experienced a change of heart. One of the boys who accompanied me to a neighboring settlement told me that he had heard of the Gospel of Jesus from Brother Wiles, but at the time he did not heed it. But now he has changed his mind and wants to learn more and work for Jesus. He is truly a "brand plucked from the burning." We enjoy this work which, although it calls for sacrifice in some ways, brings blessing and joy to our hearts when we know that even these are blood-bought souls. This week is the anniversary of our coming to the New Hebrides. So far I am the only one in my family who has suffered from malaria. But I am feeling much better now that the hot season is about over.

Milton Smith, the younger son, later described this first house: "It was a round, thatched one with an opening between the wall and the roof for breeze circulation in the hot weather. This also proved to be an invitation to interested on-lookers to view what was happening inside the house, to see how the white missionary and his family lived. Quite often mother would look up and see a head looking over the wall, watching as she worked about the house."

TALES FROM TONMIEL

Milton goes on to relate other interesting experiences.

> At the time there was no water supply. There [were] no fresh-water creeks and no tanks. The only available water was when the tide went out. Then my father, with a native to help, would go down to the beach, dig a hole, and allow the water to filter through the sand into it. When there was enough they would dip the water, now reasonably free from salt, into a bucket and carry it home. There was no way to catch water off a thatched roof.
>
> Then there was the time when I nearly ended my brief existence. We had a dog which we would take with us on our boat, chained to the mast. As we arrived in our home waters, on one occasion, the dog was as anxious to get ashore as we were. Someone let him off the chain and he dashed over the side to swim ashore. I was a toddler standing nearby, and he carried

me into the water with him. The dog struck out for the shore, but I went down, for the water was deep. Father saw what happened, but he could barely swim and both of us would probably have drowned had it not been for a native who was paddling nearby in a canoe. He dived in and fished me out of the ocean and put me into the arms of my grateful parents.

Here, in order to improve our diet, we imported a cow. In fact, we imported two. In transporting a cow from another island it was not easy to coax a wary and nervous land animal of this size into a small boat. She preferred the water to this unsure footing. So we had to drag her swimming through the water quite a distance. But we did get her on board, holding her with ropes. Then on arrival there was the problem of getting her to jump out of the boat and into the water. This is not a cow's custom. She was both afraid to jump over the side, and frightened of the water. So she had to be dragged, pushed, and virtually thrown into the water.

On another occasion Dad brought home a young bull, a wild animal securely tied to three men as they took him ashore, up the beach and into the paddock. When they let him loose, he charged at those who were around. The natives scattered in different directions, some running up trees. Dad appeared to be the one most available, so the bull took after him. There was no tree and no fence, but there was a ditch. The bull was catching up on Dad. Just as Dad jumped high to clear the ditch, the bull charged. He caught Dad and threw him back onto the bull's back, and Dad rode for quite a few yards before he slid off and the bull went on.

CHAPTER 12

SMALL CRAFT IN HEAVY SEAS

Superintendent Parker thought it was time to have a "General Meeting" of mission workers, converts, and any others who wished to come. He decided to hold this at the headquarters on the island of Atchin. This meant the calling of missionaries Ross James and wife from Santo, Don Nicholson and wife from Ambrym, the Smiths from Malekula, native teachers from various missions, and converts from heathenism and other representative natives who would come. Sea travel between these islands was more than an afternoon's outing, especially with a loaded launch; for each mission leader brought his teachers and people. Ross James's party left from Santo for Atchin, and he tells about the crossing:

> We left at daylight on Wednesday morning. We were carried ten miles out of our course with the tide, and had to spend the Sabbath on the island of Vao. It rained most of the time we were there, and we were glad to get away on Sunday morning. On Saturday night it had started to blow, and it blew hard for over a week. After reaching Atchin we decided to go to Malekula and bring the Smiths with the teacher, representatives from Tonmiel, and the Big Nambus chief and some of his men. We returned with twenty people on a twenty-foot launch. It was a battle against the strong winds and high seas. It was so rough, in fact, that we put most of the passengers ashore to walk the last three miles to the coast opposite to Atchin. Just as we were rounding the point, the dinghy broke away. We got hold of it again, but it was a difficult undertaking. It was dark by the time

we reached Atchin. The Atchin people took canoes across to Malekula to bring the Big Nambus and others across from [the] Malekula mainland. We had a few days together in this gathering, well filled with meetings, which all appreciated. Then we made our way home.

On the return trip we had heavy seas and engine trouble; also rain squalls, all of which hindered our progress. As we reached the middle of Malo Pass, South Santo, the rigging carried away. The mast broke and tore up the decking as it fell. It would have gone into the sea, sail and all, but for the halyards, which tightened and kept the sail and mast just above the waves. If I had cut the sail away it would have been lost. The whole situation was awkward and difficult. We could not leave things as they were. The engine stopped again, so without mast and with a sick engine, we decided to go back to the island for shelter, replace the mast, and attend to our engine troubles. This we did. Needless to say we were all pleased to get home again, and are not ecstatic about going down to the sea again, at least not for the present.

CANNIBALS COME TO CAMP MEETING

That the Big Nambus chief with four of his men, former notorious cannibals, should attend camp meeting may seem incredible. But this really happened when Ross James brought his party to the "General Meeting" on Atchin, and then went on to Malekula to bring the Smiths, the native teacher, people from the Tonmiel mission, and the Big Nambus chief with four of his men. These Big Nambus men were invited so that they could get some insight into how the Christians lived and what they talked about at meetings such as this. True, these heathen wanted to be taken home after the first day, but there was no way. They were virtually captive on Atchin, for no boats were leaving till the meetings were over. C. H. Parker wrote,

> Our General Meeting has come and gone. It all seems like a dream as it came and went too quickly. We had expected a Union Conference representative, but we were disappointed in this, so were left to ourselves and to God. He did not fail us. In addition to the believers on Atchin, we had fifty of our native representatives present, among whom were the Big Nambus chief Malun Vau Vau and four of his men. Both Europeans and natives felt they were well repaid coming. Our youth and children had special meetings, also the women, as the native custom is for women to meet separately from men. After the first day the Big Nambus wanted us to take them back, as they felt that if they stayed they would get under the

influence, and that if, on their return they killed pigs and carried on their heathen rites God would destroy them. However, they stayed until a day after the meetings closed, and were much softened.

The missionaries fed the natives on yams and rice. Reports from the various missions were given. All were encouraged as they listened to the dramatic experiences and conversions from heathenism. "We workers arranged to meet at midday in our different districts to pray for one another, for the work, and for special cases." Then they returned to their home islands.

In 1924, Will Smith wrote, "It is wonderful how God has overruled and ended the fighting here. For some four years the bushmen have kept these people in fear, living in dread of the surrounding bushmen who take life wholesale. Now there is a definite understanding that the fighting is finished. For this we praise the Lord. I believe the very bushmen who have been so busy in the killing will soon be seeking to find life rather than taking it. We expect soon to enter doors that have been locked to us." It is very rare for people steeped in heathen customs to voluntarily leave it, but this actually happened on Malekula. The fighting tribes decided to leave the Tonmiel people out of their fighting program, as they would not fight anyway. Pastor Smith wrote,

> It is hard to explain how these conditions came about. I do not understand myself. Suffice it to say that the Lord has heard and answered our prayers. It was just last week that our hearts were gladdened by a visit from some natives from Malua Bay, about four miles south of Tonmiel. They told us of their desire to have a teacher in their midst to teach them the way of life. They are a good class of natives, if appearance goes for anything. They came down again yesterday anxious to worship with us on the Sabbath—rank heathen in search of something better. They had already started to clear the land and build a house for the teacher.

This was a purely spontaneous effort on the part of these heathen who were dissatisfied with their way of life and searching for something better. Heathen natives are not devoid of the dignity of thinking. It was their thinking in the gloom of their pagan night that caused them to compare their lot with the Christian's, come out of the dark, and seek a better way.

FACING LOADED MUSKETS

Malekula and muskets went together in those pioneering days. The mood of the bushmen was to pull the trigger at the slightest opposition—or for no reason at

all. "The enemy does not attack the people here on points of doctrine as in the homeland," Smith wrote.

> His method is with the threat to kill. We have been greatly impressed with the fearlessness of those who have been the target of the enemy. One man in another part of the island who decided to accept Christianity and influence others to do the same, has literally stood before the loaded musket in his missionary endeavors. More than once his life has been threatened, but he has been wonderfully protected. The chief who gave the orders to shoot two of our men, died himself the next day. Many of the people looked upon his death as a stroke from God, as he was resisting the work of the Lord.

From the town of Baiap, the main town of Ambrym—Don Nicholson's island parish—came four of the strongest teachers on Malekula. Native missionaries to their fellow islanders can get closer to their own kind than the white worker can. Though outsiders may think them undereducated, they become powerful evangelists and have proved courageous in the face of death.

"From the town of Baiap have come our strongest mission helpers," wrote J. E. Fulton.

> Robert and Massignale, Joel and Joe, all from Baiap, have come as volunteer missionaries to the darker and more heathen Malekula, the most savage island. They did not have to leave their own island. It is a land of plenty, and Malekula was an enemy land where they could gain nothing of this world's goods, and were always in danger of losing their lives. The language and customs differed from those of their own island. They were teachers of a faith which condemned the heathen religion and cannibal practices, and placed them at variance with the majority. They thus came into sharp conflict with the witch doctors, who are usually jealous for the old-time religion. Often these men resort to poisoning any who oppose them.
>
> Joel and Joe were threatened again and again. More than once muskets were leveled at them, but it appeared that a restraining hand held back the assassins. Their faith in God led them on, and as of old, "subdued men," stopped the bullets, and through faith, again these simple natives "waxed valiant in fight, and turned to flight the armies of the aliens." One day Joel and others went to Espiegles Bay, and on their return Joe, weary with the walk, went down to the water hole near the beach for a drink and wash. On returning to his house it was found that he had passed within six feet of the wild bushmen who were hunting his head, waiting for him in the

tall grass. Yet these men, when they seemed to have Joel in their power, were for some unknown reason, held back from shooting. He passed them, and a moment later, when they were discovered, they fired a volley into Joel's house; but shot no one, and "the aliens took their flight." Who held them back from shooting him? Is not this a miracle of grace? Just out of heathenism, and now facing bullets for the Lord's sake?

Joe, the brother of Joel, has been located on Malua Bay, a place notorious for fierce native people. Terrible deeds have been performed here. Both Europeans and natives have been killed in this place. Yet a native not long out of darkness himself, leaves his island home and risks his life in an endeavor to bring these people to Christ.

DECOYED INTO THE ENEMIES' CAMP

Joe was threatened many times; but he moved in and out among the natives without fear, desiring no worldly favors, only asking the privilege to tell them the gospel story. He even ventured inland among his enemies. On one occasion he was invited still further inland by one who seemed to be his friend. Not suspecting the hypocrisy back of the invitation, Joe set out with Harry, an earnest native adherent. When they reached the town, the sullenness of some made them suspect that all was not well. Appearing at the chief's house they found most of the village men each holding a rifle. Without ceremony, the chief cried out, "Shoot him! Shoot him!" The men leveled their muskets to fire, when a friendly and influential native threw himself in front of Joe, crying, "Don't shoot him! He's my friend, and if you shoot him, you shoot me first, and trouble will follow."

The chief still called for Joe's death, but the men let their guns down, and Joe and Harry quietly retired, going home another way. As Joe told his story, "God closed the lions' mouths so that they did not hurt Daniel, and God has saved me from these savage people, who were cannibals and would have devoured me like lions."

CHAPTER 13

NATIVE DEFIANCE

When Will Smith took his wife and two small sons from Tonmiel to Malua Bay, he knew he was moving into a danger zone. One of the traders warned Smith not to trust the bushmen and the people at Malua Bay. "You aren't safe here for a moment," he said, "at least from any human viewpoint. The bush tribes will shoot you when you least expect it."

"I'm glad," replied Smith, "that I don't have to view the matter from a human standpoint. If I did, I'm afraid my courage would fail me. This is certainly a dangerous place, but where darkness and sin abound, grace abounds much more."

LIVING DANGEROUSLY

Everyone lived dangerously in this trigger-happy territory; murder and revenge were a way of life. Whole tribes would take sides in a single murder incident, and war would follow. At Malua Bay, Suan's father was shot by a man of the Tinambet tribe of the Big Nambus. For Suan and his brother, this was a tragedy that must be avenged. Bill, chief of the Tinambet, advised the boys not to make trouble with him but to go kill the killer himself. When they had done their murder, they called out to the chief from a distance: "We did what you said. Now that we have avenged our father, the trouble is finished here and we are going down to join the mission."

But the trouble was not finished there. A payback was required of the boys who killed the previous murderer. The Tinambet tribe threatened the tribe now at the mission and declared war on the mission itself. This was the most serious

situation the Smith family had ever faced. These were Big Nambus bushmen, without scruples when on the warpath. There was no way of escape; the Smiths had no launch at that time. The natives who had built their houses around the mission still had weapons, and they swore to protect the mission family. The brothers, with other members of their tribe, took a keen interest in the teachings of the mission, attending worship both morning and evening. When reports came through that trouble was brewing, the mission people were nervous and watched night and day. Morning worship was held when the sun was well up, and evening worship long before it set, lest they should be taken by surprise by men stalking in the shadows.

The Smiths' house was built on an elevation a short distance from the beach, and the cow paddock was down near the beach. One morning early, as was his routine, Will took his bucket and went to milk the cow, passing through tall grass beside the path. Halfway down to the beach, Will was startled by a wild bushman who rose suddenly out of the grass with a musket, cocked and pointed straight at him. Will thought his last moment on earth had come. But the native, speaking in pidgin English, said, "Master, you listen to me. You stop, go back to mission. We are fighting only your black boys."

Will forgot about the cow and took the advice of the native. He started back up the hill, but had gone only a few steps when he heard a rifle shot, then more shots. At the mission house he found the chief of the mission tribe, Lilitil, lying at his front door, shot in the abdomen with his internal organs blown out, writhing in pain.

When the first shot was fired, Lilitil heard a woman cry out, "Oh, the master is shot." He snatched up his rifle and ran down the path to protect Pastor and Mrs. Smith. At the front door he received the death wound. The other men at the mission rushed out and aimed their muskets at the fleeing forms of those who had done the shooting. But a marvelous thing happened: There was a click of triggers, but not one of their muskets fired, and the killers got away unharmed. Afterward it was learned that some two hundred Big Nambus men waited below to avenge the death of any of their tribesmen. This would have meant the killing of everyone at the mission, including the missionary family. "Who kept those cartridges from exploding?" wrote Parker in his report. "Brother Smith sent word off to me at once, and in three hours I was anchored at Malua Bay. They took me to the place in the path on the way up to the village and showed me a twig tied to a tree close to the path. 'Do you know what it means?' they asked. I shook my head, No. The natives explained: 'The chief of the Tinambet and his men say, "We defy God. We defy the government. We defy the mission. We are strong, and God, the

government and the mission are nothing. We are able to blot all of you out of existence. You listen well to our talk." '

"Our native people were all discouraged," wrote Parker, "and wanted us to take them to some other place. They said, 'If we stay here we are all dead men.' Brother Smith and I knew that if we gave up the station there, the Tonmiel people would be next. Then the Matanavat mission would go, and then Wo Wo, which would mean the annihilation of our work on Malekula."

Parker continued, "Brother and Sister Smith rose to the occasion and said they would not leave." The Sabbath came, and Pastor Smith had a special message for the anxious people. It became a rebaptism of faith, hope, and courage. They were all weeping together when Harry, who had been shot, stood up and said, "I am ready to die for my Master Jesus. I will be a martyr for my Lord, and I will never leave this place unless I am carried off dead." Manoa, his brother, expressed himself in the same way.

A DRAMATIC CHANGE

Just then Pastor Smith looked out of the door and froze in fear. He saw several dusky forms moving back and forth outside. He thought they were surrounded by bushmen, who would kill them all at once. There was only one thing to do—call on the Lord for deliverance.

Then came a surprise! Instead of intending violence, the savages, representing a large tribe of bush people, had been watching the lives of those on the mission and had decided they wanted this way of life too. They had come to talk with Pastor Smith about locating their new village around the mission site so that they could have a school and learn the way of worship. Not only this, but they were friends of the Big Nambus chief and offered to mediate between them and the threatening Tinambet tribe.

C. H. Parker continues his account:

> While this tribe was still talking, another chief and his people came down, and matters were soon arranged, and word taken to the chief of the Tinambet tribe. In response to the mediation, that same afternoon several men of the Tinambet tribe came down to see Brother Smith. They now told him he had nothing to fear, that this was a black man's trouble, and nothing more. They told him that their chief would be glad to see him, that he would be perfectly safe, and they would provide him a bodyguard.
>
> These Tinambet tribesmen further told Pastor Smith that they did not want him to leave, but wished him to stay. God has wonderfully changed

the dark conditions, and let His presence shine into the hearts of these people, lighting up the gloom. The Smiths have manifested a wonderful degree of courage, faith, and perseverance. Through God's help they have saved the situation on Malekula.

SUBMITTING TO A WEIRD CUSTOM

While the Smiths were on furlough in Australia, missionary Don Nicholson visited Malekula and reported,

> Landing on these hostile shores gives one a strange feeling—there is uncertainty and the possibility of death; a feeling of utter helplessness among depraved men. After making friends and shaking hands, we usually had to submit to these cannibal people's custom. While I was seated in the midst of a large company of men and boys, the chief took hold of my arms, my legs, and then my body, gently gripping the fleshy parts, and uttering a deep "Uuh, uuh." Turning to the Tonmiel chief, he asks, "What does this man eat? He is the fattest man I have yet seen." The teacher responded, "He does not eat much, only bread and fruit; and he drinks water." Again the deep, guttural "Uuh, uuh." Following this, each man and each boy had the privilege of doing as his chief had done.
>
> During this time all I could do was to sit and smile and join in a few words with his chief counselor, who knew some English. One of our Tonmiel boys became alarmed and fled back to our ship during the ordeal. Harry, the Tonmiel teacher, said he felt sick at heart during these proceedings, and as he listened to their conversation about human flesh, he wondered if they had not made a mistake in asking to come ashore.
>
> Now the conversation turned to the missions. The chief asked why we had not come before, and assured me he wanted a mission to locate in their midst. He said he was prepared to leave his bush home and come down with his people to the shore, where they would place themselves under direction of the mission. He said another chief would join with him and move his village to the right side of the ground he proposed to give as a mission site. He also had hopes of the powerful Amok tribe coming down and building a new village in the rear, and still another tribe building on the left. Through his counselors he laid out these careful plans before us.
>
> "Is this a genuine move," I asked him, "seeing so much fighting in the district?" He looked me straight in the eye and said, "I am the chief of the

Ninimbus, and if I give my word, nothing can change it."

His counselor has great confidence in Christianity, and assured me he believed it is the only thing that can save his people. The chief said they wanted to give up cannibalism and fighting. They wanted medical assistance and someone to care for their young people. So while they come in their ignorance, in their heathenism and cannibalism, the Tonmiel have shown them a way of life which they envy and are anxious to have.

NATIVE FAITHFULNESS

Heathen opposition to the gospel can be violent and threatening, using both arguments and muskets. It may result in the surrounding of a mission, as happened three times to early Adventist missionaries on Atchin, or it may lead to some irresponsible killing. So it was with some misgivings that the Smiths left the believers to the hands of their indigenous teachers while they went on furlough. However, on returning they found that some of the most unlikely ones had been faithful, in spite of heavy pressures to return to their heathenism.

> The very people we thought could not hold out against the opposition of their heathen neighbors have come right into the mission and forsaken their former life. One man, a chief who objected to the idea of a mission when we were here last year, has in our absence, identified himself with our people at Malua Bay. Others who returned to their heathen homes because of threats to wipe them out, mission and all, have retraced their steps and are numbered among our company. What a God we serve, and what gratitude we have as we see how He has answered our prayers!

WINNING THE WILDEST OF MEN

Will Smith was elated, and he had reason to be. He was seeing human metamorphosis, the dramatic transformation of grisly killers and cannibals into kind, lovable Christians. There was excitement in his writings when conversions of this kind took place. "It has been our privilege," he wrote,

> to see with our eyes things almost beyond comprehension. We have seen men and women, who from early childhood have been held by the cruel chains of Satan, now made free indeed through Christ Jesus. We have waited for years to see the very things that we see just now. Last Sabbath

my wife and I had cause for great rejoicing as we sat in our new native church building and listened to men and women say, with tears in their eyes, that they were giving themselves to Jesus. One old man with trembling voice told how he had been responsible for the death of many people. Two men testified that they had killed and eaten men, but now they were giving their lives to God.

Pastor Smith wrote of a baptism of seventeen on October 29, 1928, with headhunters, cannibals, wife beaters, and thieves among those baptized. They gave evidence of genuine conversion and were strictly instructed in the knowledge of the gospel. He mentioned twenty-four actual church members at Malua Bay, but of course there were many more adherents associated with the mission.

NATIVE TEACHERS

The native teachers are the frontline workers to their own indigenous people. In the early days of missions, they risked assassinations at the hands of resentful heathen. As mentioned earlier, five teachers for the Presbyterian mission were killed and eaten. These teachers are to their people living in the heart of heathenism what the minister is to his church in the homeland, except for the primitive, dangerous conditions.

Native teachers are recruited from their native villages. Promising young men are invited to come to Aore Training School, where they are given a basic education and training in the Bible. After a year or two they may be sent out to some mission station, then brought back periodically for further training. One of these teachers, Meluk Woraim, testified, "When Mr. Smith and Mr. Broad came to Atchin to get students for the training school, I did not want to go. They talked with me, but I did not care. My heart was so unwilling to listen that I went away and hid myself. That went on for some time, but the Holy Spirit changed me altogether, and made me say one morning, 'All right, I too will go to Aore for training.' Now if God can make me willing to go where I did not want to go, I know He must be true." This was an unexpected testimony; the missionaries knew nothing of the struggle that took place in the heart of this boy.

CHAPTER 14

MANY A DANGER

A startling radio message reached Australia on July 4, 1929: "Ambrym blew up Friday night. Craig's Cove, Baiap mission completely destroyed. No lives lost. Advise relatives."

Ambrym is a volcanic island with several craters. The flow of molten lava had obliterated the missions on the southeast side of the island. Baiap Mission Station, the most prosperous, had been opened by two native young men. Pastor and Mrs. Don Nicholson had fostered this work, and finally Mr. and Mrs. Taylor were stationed there. It was a beautiful station, with everything laid out symmetrically, but it was in the line of the lava flow now and the Taylors' home was soon engulfed. When Mr. Taylor saw the approaching lava, he called his native boys, who quickly passed the news on to the community. Hastily the missionaries caught up their nineteen-month-old baby and fled to a point on the coast about four miles distant, where they passed the night in the bush under heavy rain. The next morning Mr. Taylor returned in a trader's launch to see the damage and found no sign of his house. As the launch approached Craig's Cove, the lava entered the sea for the first time. In less than half an hour the water was hot two miles out. When he visited the island two weeks later, he found that the entire mission station had disappeared—buried under twelve feet of lava. Of the fifteen houses in the native village, only two were left.

Some lives were reported lost in a native village inland, where a few blind and maimed people were left to perish.

ANOTHER NARROW ESCAPE

Will Smith almost ended his earthly sojourn one night in the Pacific Ocean. As he told it,

> Brother W. O. Broad and I started out on my launch from Aore to take some Ambrymese students home for the school vacation. All went well until we reached Bushman's Bay, when the engine refused to work. We were at anchor at the time, and succeeded in replacing a broken spring in the magneto. We had not gone far when the spring broke again, and although we put in another, the engine would not run. We went in search of another launch to take us to Ambrym, and were able to find one.
>
> I had for some time wanted to visit Ambrym, but had been hindered, so I accompanied the man who had charge of this cutter. He is a skilled seaman, having been in this line for nineteen years. His boat's crew consisted of three Big Nambus men and one Atchinese. We met rather rough tides toward the coast of Ambrym, and had to take great care. I paid a good visit to our Baiap and Yinmek missions, and then went on to Limbul and Olao, where we anchored. That night we spent on the cutter, but the sea was so rough that we slept very little. Next day I visited more of our missions around the north shore of Ambrym, and it was agreed that I should stay there for the night. But on returning to the ship at 4:30 p.m. he said that we must go, as the sea was rising and the ship had dragged her anchor. About midnight we were on the way, the moon giving us good light for a time. Having had a rather strenuous week, and being unable to get the rest I needed, I was grateful for the prospect of sleep.
>
> Somewhere in the early morning hours, after the moon had set and a good while before daylight, for some reason I slipped off the top of the cabin where I was sleeping, suddenly finding myself in the sea. I wakened as if in a dream, only to find that the boat was traveling on and on, leaving me behind. I shouted and shouted. Of course with the tremendous thump of the engine and the boat going at such a speed, it was in vain for me to shout. How I struggled in the water and strained my eyes to see if that boat would turn or just go on. How I prayed and fought to get where they might hear my voice. But oh, what a loving Father we serve! Within a few minutes, in spite of the fact that the men on the ship could not see or hear me in the water, the ship turned around and headed straight back for me. When they came alongside I shouted, and they heard my voice, stopped the engine, and lowered the sail.

Not being a strong swimmer, I was almost exhausted by this time. Except for divine intervention, I must have gone down in only a minute or two. The dinghy came and they picked me up. In their hurry to get the dinghy down into the water, it filled, and this prolonged my stay in the sea. My clothes made it difficult to hold out. I must have been in the water twelve to eighteen minutes. I had just sufficient strength to get into the dinghy, but praise God I did, and into the boat also.

THEN THE FEVER

Immediately I got my wet clothes off, I shook like a leaf, and although I had not had malaria for about a year, it immediately seized me. It is quite possible that the fever was upon me before I rolled off the cutter. Sometimes it comes on just like that, and one wakes up in a kind of nightmare to find the fever present. Those who have been malaria subjects know how absolutely helpless the fever renders one while it is on, and this may account for the mishap.

On arriving home, the full force of the fever came upon me. That was Friday, and Sabbath and Sunday I was very helpless, but here it is Monday and I am beginning to feel myself again, having been brought within one step of death.

Sometime later, Smith nearly died of the blackwater fever brought on by malaria. Pastor Smith added that the miracle of the rescue was not lost on the boat's crew and particularly the captain. They were not Christians, but it sobered them somewhat, as they sensed that finding him in the dark and other features of the deliverance were more than a coincidence.

CHAPTER 15

THE FRUIT OF MISSIONS

Pastor C. H. Parker returned to supervise the work in the New Hebrides after the departures of Ross James and Will Smith. As soon as possible the missionaries planned a camp meeting that all workers and as many people as possible would attend. Pastors A. G. Stewart and W. G. Turner were delegated by the Australasian Union Conference as visiting ministers from Australia. They arrived early enough to visit the missions before the meetings began so that they could become familiar with the work in progress. The sedate Pastor Turner was highly intrigued when, on Malekula, some of the bushmen pinched him over many parts of his body and exhibited shock and dismay when they noticed his gold tooth. How to grow a single gold tooth was too much of a mystery for them. They must have a second and third look at this singular phenomenon; besides, he was the only white man that grew gold teeth. Turner did not say how they solved the mystery. "It was rather embarrassing," he wrote, "but they were simply like curious children."

Pastor Turner continued describing his trip:

> We sailed in the evening for Malua Bay, where we have a fine mission. This is where Will Smith had been stationed. From here the next morning we commenced our walk to the Tinambet people, a tribe of Small Nambus natives. After at least three hours' walk over rough country we reached their village, to find most of the people away or recovering from a big feast at which 700 pigs had been slaughtered. We gathered those villagers that

we could and held a service with them, pinning the picture roll to one of their drums. The young people seemed interested, and at this village we found it possible to approach the womenfolk, although here, as elsewhere, they were poor, frightened, and oppressed.

Returning to Malua Bay in time for Sabbath, we opened the day with the natives in their church. On this mission we found over seventy people residing. Among the women were many whose front upper teeth had been knocked out according to their custom when they were heathen, while we met one woman who had buried her child alive as do the heathen. The next day at 8:00 p.m. we boarded the boat (the *Le Phare,* a new mission vessel) with Jack Radley as captain, and headed for Ambrym. After an all-night run we reached Baiap, once the most beautiful of our missions, but now the most desolate following the volcano's eruption. A number of our people have moved from the lava bed and built houses nearby. Joe, a fine teacher, is stationed here, and about sixty adults reside at the mission.

Later in the day we visited among the heathen villages of North Ambrym. Here we met the paramount chief, Tahinmal Malur, a very old man who claims to have met Captain Cook. He describes Cook's ship and proudly shows a piece of steel given him to make an axe. As Captain Cook called at the New Hebrides 150 years ago, we had serious doubts about his story. The chief's son is a regular attendant at the mission.

At times, we called in some of our leading native teachers to discuss certain features of the work, and found them fine, intelligent, thinking men. Personally I think we have material in the New Hebrides equal to that found anywhere in the Western Pacific. As our teachers reported and spoke of experiences in prayer and victory gained, we realized that they possess the knowledge of a personal Saviour and the consciousness of a prayer-hearing God.

TESTIMONY OF OFFICIALS, TRADERS, AND NATIVES

Missionaries are not always appreciated. Often they are criticized for interfering with the natives' way of life. It was refreshing, therefore, for Pastor W. G. Turner, of the Australasian Union Conference of Seventh-day Adventists, to receive warm commendation from British and French government officials, white traders, and natives themselves. Turner wrote, "The same work of transformation wrought by the power of God in other lands is seen in the New Hebrides today. These changes are remarked upon by all classes within the group of

islands. White traders praised the high standard of our work. The natives themselves discuss it, and as we called on French and British Government officials, they quite freely told us they were impressed with the results of our mission work. We found the residents of the group supporting us and calling for us to commence work in other parts of the field."

Mr. William C. Grove, research fellow in social anthropology for the Australasian Research Council, visited certain Seventh-day Adventist missions in the Pacific, but not out of love for missions, for he knew very little about them. He was interested in studying the effect of European culture upon the natives, and he chose Adventist missions because they were of easy access. Writing in one *Sydney Morning Herald*, he told of his visit to the islands of Mussau and Emirau, off the coast of New Guinea.

> I was no friend of the S.D.A. mission. I mean, I had no special desire to further their cause. I simply wanted to see just what was happening, and how to evaluate the work from the point of view of present social and economic and future development. From the moment we dropped anchor at Emirau, I knew that the Seventh-day mission had these people; knew unmistakably with my own eyes, that here was no decadent people, here no racial malaise such as I had recently seen in parts of New Ireland. Here we met old Naphtali, a fine, honest, hard-working Fijian teacher, and saw the whole island's population hurriedly and excitedly gathering together at the point of the beach where our dinghy was landing us. It was a moment of enthusiasm and joyous welcome.
>
> I soon got off among the natives alone, by themselves in their settlement. From every angle I approached them—trying suggestions, cajolery, ridicule upon individuals and groups. Fast they stood, fast for a new life, with no regrets, and, as far as I could see, no possible ill effects on their social or economic lives. In fact, in the latter connection, I found that under Naphtali's leadership they had abundance of food, including varieties previously unknown. I was particularly struck with the faithfulness of the Solomon Island teachers—such black-skinned joyous types as Oti, whose genuine Christian belief was apparent in his every action. Truly the S.D.A. stations will become, have become already, the focal points of new interests, radiating centers of new life.
>
> Improved housing and village hygiene may be expected as a result of mission's example and teaching. What indeed may the S.D.A. Mission not accomplish among these people, to the lasting credit of the mission and the salvation of what was a decadent society, if it proceeds along these lines

of enlightenment and understanding? What a unique opportunity has the S.D.A. Mission at Mussau and Emirau, starting in these days of educational enlightenment, to show all other organizations the way.

ATCHIN EVIDENCE

A fine example in the New Hebrides of practical value of the Adventist mission program is the church built on Atchin wholly by native labor. It was of modern construction with material all brought over from Australia. Not only did the Atchinese people build it, but they saved money from copra sales and worked on plantations and trading ships to earn the money to buy the material. It cost them some $16,000, and at best they would be paid two dollars a day.

The population of Atchin is barely 600, and the church is built to seat 300. At the dedication 800 were present—traders, government officials, and chiefs and visitors from other missions. These were lavish in their praise for the Adventist mission program. One Frenchman remarked that it was beyond all other efforts for the natives. A builder for another mission said, "If we could get our boys to work like this it would be wonderful. I have to do it all myself; my boys do not know one end of the saw from another."

Pastor Stewart recalled the words of a police superintendent when he first arrived on Atchin: "If you can make any impression on these people in twenty years you will be doing well." And he exclaimed, as he had often done in the intervening years, "What hath God wrought!"

CHAPTER 16

A NEW GENERATION TAKES OVER

Pastor C. H. Parker was the first of the Adventist pioneers to arrive in the New Hebrides and the last pioneer to leave, twenty-two years later. How much was accomplished during that time! Of course, this was a combined effort also involving the Harold Carrs, A. G. Stewarts, Norman Wileses, Will Smiths, Ross Jameses, and Don Nicholsons.

The new mission superintendent appointed to these islands was Pastor G. H. Engelbrecht. After his initial survey of his new field, he wrote, "There is a strong interest in the 'Sabbath Mission' among the natives of practically every island, and many anxiously await the day when we shall be able to place teachers among them. At present we have over forty native teachers in the field, of whom we are justly proud. The writer has just returned from Tanna, where a wonderful work has grown up during the past three years. Eleven village schools are being conducted here continuously."

Later he reported, "Attendance at the thirty-five Sabbath schools in the New Hebrides has now reached 1,129. The majority have daily lesson study with their teachers morning by morning. Nine hundred attend Youth meetings regularly. The baptized membership of the churches now stands at 525, with 56 baptisms for the year. Total contributions to the cause from all sources, including tithe, 623 pounds. The mission conducts village and training schools throughout the territory, 400 students being in attendance in 1939. The working force of this field, of whom six are white missionaries, now numbers 44."

MALEKULA STILL UNTAMED

"The one sad spot in it all is Malekula," he added. "At the present time the work in this part is almost at a standstill. Our last visit to the Big Nambus was at the end of March, 1940. In the previous October, a recruiter, Mr. Paul Mazoyer, was murdered by some of these people, and the Government has issued an order forbidding any launch or ship to call upon them. We have eighteen stations on Tanna and only eleven teachers."

Even as the decade of the fifties began, many parts of Malekula still showed the sordid side of heathenism. Many natives had broken away from their inland tribes, escaped their degraded environment, and set up new homes in Christian communities around mission stations. They could not live Christian lives amidst the heathen influences, because of the natural resentment held by the tribes that had abandoned Christianity. Sooner or later the Christians came under threat of death. No excuse was needed, just the whims of a trigger-happy heathen.

Missionary C. T. Parkinson told of an event in 1955 that sounded like the old Malekula.

> The hollow tones of the tomtoms echoed somewhat mournfully along the northwest coast of Malekula. It was time for Sabbath School to begin, and church members from Tonmeil and Matanavat moved into their seats. The first hymn was being sung. Outside, Kenneth, a lad of twelve, was hurrying from Tonmeil to Matanavat. He had come two miles, and this morning he was late. Two hundred yards from the church, already within the sound of hymns, men hiding in the bush fired at him. The shot found its mark, shattering the boy's right arm, tearing across his chest, and entering his left arm. He fell to the ground and his assailants fled.
>
> In the church the hymn ended abruptly as everyone rushed outside. They looked in the direction from which the shot had come, and saw Kenneth making his way to meet them. Blood was flowing freely from his gaping wounds. He fell down, got up laboriously and struggled on, only to collapse and die at their feet, murdered for no apparent reason. As to who killed the innocent lad, no one knows and perhaps no one ever will. This is the third time in a year that killings have taken place on the north coast of Malekula.

"Along this coastline," Parkinson continued, "we have seven companies; four of these are in the country of the Little Nambus. Except for our village along this coastal fringe the people are heathen, and classified by the government as

'not under control of government authority.' Our work for them has now continued for a long time, and we have made but small inroads. In the eyes of the bush people it is immaterial whether the person killed is Christian or heathen. All that matters is that he is either Little or Big Nambus."

BIG NAMBUS THREATENS DESTRUCTION

In 1958, Pastor O. D. F. McCutcheon was president of the New Hebrides Mission. He cabled the following to Pastor G. Branster, president of the Central Pacific Mission: "Because Big Nambus threaten[s] destruction [to] villages [on] their coast, we in conjunction [with] government have evacuated our people from dangers. Re Malekula, Tonmaru village burning. Evacuating more northern villages. No casualties yet."

Branster reported to the Australian headquarters the following:

> The island of Malekula is the most primitive and heathen section of our field. Our people have been working among these people for many years, but they are still untamed, and authorities seem unable to keep them in order. Several thousand of them live in the mountains. They are big, strapping men, but wily and well supplied with guns and ammunition, which they receive from unscrupulous traders. As the years have passed, some have come down and built new villages along the coast. Various episodes of shootings have taken place. The deacon of one of our churches was shot dead one Friday afternoon while gathering food from his garden in preparation for Sabbath. Following this episode the government closed this area to visitors for a period; but things appeared to have quieted down, and some of the tribes are becoming more friendly.
>
> It is now evident that the devil is fermenting trouble among the Malekulans, and they have come down in force, determined to wipe out the coastal villages under the mission's control. Please pray with us that the Lord will protect the lives of our missionaries and people.

CHAPTER 17

THE SIGNIFICANT SIXTIES

As the decade began, Malekula was still a primitive place, with a reputation for danger and lawlessness. When it came to tourists and visiting officials, Malekula stole the show, for all wanted to see the notorious Nambus, or man-eaters. An Italian photographic party, having heard of these colorful cannibals, came loaded with cameras to get some rare pictures. They plodded up the mountain path into the territory of the bush people, and the "shots" they got were of the wrong kind—coming their way from the Nambuses' guns. The photographers learned that this was the native way of saying, "Trespassers Prosecuted, Keep Out!" The party retreated without so much as a glimpse of the musket-happy Malekulans.

TRANSFER OF HEADQUARTERS

During this decade the Adventist mission headquarters was transferred to Santo. Until 1930, the Adventist center had been on the island of Atchin, off the coast of northern Malekula. It was from here that Parker, Stewart, Wiles, James, and Smith reached out to the other islands. Then Aore, an island off the south coast of Santo, was bought for 600 pounds, and new headquarters were established there in 1930. Pastor A. C. Thomson, president of the New Hebrides Mission in 1961, tells how things were developed in the Islands.

> Thirteen years ago, when I landed in the New Hebrides, the mission headquarters was situated on Aore, an island in the northern section of the

group. Santo, the nearest shipping center, could boast only four stores, a hospital, a post office in the French Delegate's office, and a great deal of material and building left by the U. S. Armed Forces. The ship from Australia arrived every six weeks.

There had been little change since the mission had transferred its headquarters from Atchin. Providentially, Aore was selected and obtained. The work on this large estate grew. Today the mission buildings include the Parker Missionary School with 153 students, the Aore workshop and slipway, and the New Seventh-day Adventist Hospital. As this development has continued and the membership increased—from 430 in 1948 to 1,560 in 1961—the administrative section has grown with various departments. For a number of years the office has been the front room and veranda of the president's home.

Santo has also expanded and its population increased. It now boasts the only modern store in the New Hebrides, plus many other stores. A modern wharf, also the only one in the group, attracts about six ships per month with cargo from different countries. Three plane services now operated through Santo, one of them twice weekly. So at the 1959 Mission Session it was decided to transfer headquarters to this center. It is almost impossible to purchase land in Santo. Prices are ridiculous for such an isolated place. However, an ideal position just off the main road was purchased for the office and church. This is right in the town area. The office is almost completed and we require finance for the house of worship. Meetings are now held in the home with as many as fifty attending. As soon as we are able to build a church we will commence regular evangelistic meetings.

RETURN OF ALMA WILES

In 1963, Alma Wiles and her sister-in-law, Mrs. Vida Harris, from Australia, paid a visit to the islands. This was Mrs. Wiles's first visit in forty-eight years. What changes she found! For five years they had labored without a single baptism, just winning the confidence of the cannibals as they could. Gathering a few primitive villagers around them, shining a light into their darkened souls, she and Norman introduced to them salvation through Christ and the promise of a more abundant way of life. But it was uphill work for those pioneers. Now, on her return, she saw something of the harvest, and she was heartened. Now there were almost one thousand baptized members. Perhaps the most striking contrast was apparent in the status of women. Before Christianity came, their lives were considered of little

worth, a dismal existence of degradation and slavery.

R. W. Taylor reports in the *South Pacific Record* that

> in all, five of those who had lived in the Wiles' household were there to welcome home the one who had brought them the good news of Jesus' love.
>
> No wonder the several hundred delegates to the meetings, representing thousands more members throughout the New Hebrides, sang praises to God with heartfelt vigour.
>
> At the sound of the singing in that opening meeting—perhaps seeing it as a foretaste of the great meeting scheduled for the "courts above"—the ageing veteran missionary, sitting up front in a seat of honor, was overcome by the scene. "It was worth it all," she said, tearfully. "If only Norman could see them now. Yes, it was worth it all."

At a mission session attended by Alma Wiles, Pastor R. E. Cobbin told of

> volunteers, receiving no remuneration whatever, making a contribution to education because of the shortage of teachers. On the last night a call was made for rededication, and 160 laymen pledged themselves to endeavor to win one in the next twelve months. Twelve laymen volunteered to enter the heathen areas still existing on the islands of Santo, Malekula and Pentecost. Among the delegates were some from our most recently entered village of Whynn on Malekula. These people are making good progress in the Christian faith and working to build a church. The delegates voted that all members of the New Hebrides Mission observe a week of sacrifice to earn money for a nurses' home, sorely needed on Aore, near the hospital.

THE CARGO CULT

A weird religious cult invaded the islands of the Pacific in the 1920s. It grew slowly at first, but swelled to alarming proportions in the 1940s, and especially after World War II. It was devastating to established Christian missions. Called the "Cargo Cult," it spread the idea that by using the white man's magic, the natives, too, could obtain the white man's wealth. "How come the white man can call up ships on the endless sea and great birds out of the open skies, all loaded with such wonderful things?" they asked. "Not only do they bring axes, knives, tomahawks and muskets, food, and clothing, but thunderous guns, jeeps, and refrigerators—all from some supernatural storehouse of the white man's gods."

The white man was never seen to pay for these things, nor work hard to make them. He obtained them free, "plenty too many," simply by talking into a box. According to the cult, the missionary has passed on to the natives the white man's religion but withheld all these wonderful things. The natives must now discover the secret of the white man's magic. They must learn how to invoke the white man's gods. Some believed that the white men were the spirits of their ancestors returning with all this stupendous cargo.

The cult was rampant in New Guinea, Solomon Islands, Fiji, New Caledonia, and New Hebrides. When 120,000 troops landed in the New Hebrides and another 200,000 in New Caledonia with all their equipment, it was mind-boggling to the primitive islanders. How we might view an invasion from Mars. Dean Giles, writing of the cult on Tanna, said that John Frum was the accepted apostle for bringing about this promised utopia, "where no hunger, sickness nor death would exist. These beliefs have resulted in bizarre conduct, such as the making of airfields in the bush and wharves on the coast for expected cargo. Dancing orgies with licentiousness were held. On Tanna the people have thrown large sums of money into the sea, believing that their needs would soon be supplied by John Frum. Every Friday night from all over the island, they congregate at Sulpher Springs to dance and carry out their rites."

This cult was, then, an attempt to make use of the white man's material civilization without his religion. Its leaders taught a strange mixture of Christian and pagan traditions, all given with instruction as to how to prepare for the supply ships to arrive. Pastor Ross James, of Santo, told of their belief in the resurrection of the dead to coincide with the arrival of the supply ships. But the white people must all be killed, and this was simply the death of the wicked.

As part of this program, their leader with one or two others went to the home of a Mr. Clapcott and asked him for a chicken and some tobacco. When his back was turned, they killed him. Five sticks were neatly placed on the family table of another home as a warning that it was now their turn. But the leader was caught and hurried on board ship, to which he did not object, for he told them they could not pull up anchor while he was on board. He was executed nevertheless.

"A strange phenomenon of the cult is its seemingly unconnected appearances. On an island, life can be very quiet and normal, then without warning some prophet appears—it may be an old man or woman—who hears a voice telling them to get ready, for the cargo is coming. After years of waiting and listening with two half coconut shells hard clamped on their ears for earphones, and talking into some small box, they become disillusioned and the cult subsides. Yet soon it will break out in another village" (Dr. H. J. Margull, *The Bible in the World*, 1965).

Both Adventists and Presbyterians lost large numbers of members to the cult. During the war years there were no missionaries on hand to meet the emergency. The leader, John Frum, remains a mystery. Overall the cult appears to be an aberration produced when the primitive mind was confronted with the technology of the Pacific war. The troops were unwittingly responsible for building huge hopes in the minds of the people, and to this day many retain the hope that John Frum will return.

Pastor Dean Giles, a missionary in the New Hebrides in the 1960s, wrote, "Happily we can report that there has been a restoration of confidence in the mission and large numbers have returned and joined the Adventist faith."

CHAPTER 18

NAMBUS STILL PRIMITIVE—A 1965 VISIT

It is ironic that the Big Nambus still remain crude and uncivilized after fifty years of contact with missionaries and an opportunity to improve their way of life. In Parker's day the mission was given land, and the chief asked for a mission. Why did they not go in? I asked Ross James, one of the pioneers.

"Too risky," he said. "Already they had killed and eaten some Presbyterian teachers; what assurance, apart from the chief's word, did we have that our teachers would not suffer the same fate?" So when the Wileses set up a mission on Malekula, it was near the coast, where with a launch they could have the safety of the sea. The government official, in giving permission for the location, advised against going into the mountain area, and time has proved the wisdom of that decision.

Eric Were gives an interesting account of a visit in 1965. Were, the Adventists' official photographer, wrote,

> In 1919 famous Kansas cameraman, Martin Johnson and his wife Osa, landed on the shores of Malekula to make the first commercial motion picture of the Big Nambus people. At that time these musket-toting bushmen were considered to be the most primitive and savage people in the world. They were notorious for the murderous raids which they made on coastal villages, and were feared far and wide.
>
> When the Johnsons arrived in the New Hebrides they found Adventist missionaries Norman and Alma Wiles and other pioneers already on

the job. Johnson took the well-known photograph of the Wiles couple sitting among the Big Nambus warriors. Not long after, Norman was struck down with blackwater fever and gave his life in service for the primitive Malekulans. Forty-five years later—last September, to be precise—I landed on those same shores, also carrying a motion-picture camera, bent on filming the Big Nambus as they are today. I was accompanied by Dr. Joeli, Fijian-born Medical Director of our Aore hospital, who was to do a medical patrol on Malekula. Our morale was boosted by the company of Pastor Dean Giles, president of the New Hebrides Mission; Bill Payntor, secretary-treasurer; and Alan White, mission director on Aoba Island.

We went ashore from the mission vessel *Leleo* at Tenmaru, and made arrangements for carriers to help us inland next morning. Soon after sunrise, with local Pastor Takau as chief guide, we set off up a steep grade along a narrow foot-trail that ran through dense bamboo thickets and brought us out onto a high, wind-swept plateau. Ahead we could see jungle-covered mountains, the hideout of the fabled Big Nambus. About this time we would hear musket shots if the tribesmen were in a mean mood, but as the hills were silent we presumed that all was well.

Our party proceeded along the trail that wound through thick jungle and skirted thirsty creeks (this was the dry season) and in about two and a half hours brought us to the village of Tenamet. This was our first contact with the famous Big Nambus people, they were dressed—or I should say, undressed—in the same manner as when first contacted so many years ago. Sullen and silent, they gave us no jovial welcome, but at least they did not shoot at us.

Dr. Joeli soon found some medical work to attend to and the people began to thaw out a little. I took advantage of the improved relations to take some pictures. We left them on friendly terms. Moving on from Tenamet, we attacked more thickly wooded country and about midday, hot and tired, we found the village of Makauwe. Here were more of the same people—bearded, lethargic old men, seemingly with little interest in life; and shy women with red-dyed head-dresses of coarse fiber and a haunted look in their eyes. Joeli dressed burns and ulcers, gave injections, and treated malaria and dysentery. We could see that the Fijian doctor was treated with great respect by these bush people.

Later in the afternoon Pastor Takau told the local chief that we would honor him by sleeping in his village that night. We were designated a house similar to the filthy, skull-lined houses we had already inspected. Our first look at Motel Makauwe was not encouraging. It had no windows and its one door was barely two feet square. You almost had to be a

contortionist to enter the place. Besides the usual filth, heaps of Kava spittings and litter, it had a huge pig tethered inside to give it a homey atmosphere. We decided to build a leafy humpy in the jungle nearby! However, Pastor Takau informed us that the chief would be highly offended if we spurned his hospitality, and we would lose ground we had gained in friendly relations. So like it or not, we joined the pig!

We were shown corners of the house where slats of wood low on the earth represented a bed. The center of the house was taken up by the local boys preparing, cooking, and eventually eating a kind of scraped yam pudding, done in banana leaves on hot stones. Our native attendants enjoyed this, but we were thankful we were not offered any of the delicacy.

After the smoke of cooking had died down we prepared for sleep. Bill Paynter had brought an air-mattress which he insisted that I, being the senior member of the party, should use. This fine gesture on Bill's part must be recorded as one of the most selfless acts of history. As a reward for his kindness, Bill drew the sleeping place nearest to the pig—his feet being within gnawing distance of old Grunter. However, the pig contented himself with chewing on some old sweet potatoes and made sundry slurps and grunts during the night. Rats in the rafters and fleas in our beds completed the motel's amenities.

We awoke early in the morning little rested. I was in fairly good shape, thanks to the air-mattress, but others had kinks in their backs that took hours to straighten out. We had a quick breakfast in the glorious out-of-doors, then headed for Amok, our last Big Nambus village. Here we found the usual medical work to do, and Takau told a story from the picture roll. Then we started the long, hot trail to the coast. We had visited the last hard-core devil worshippers of Malekula; a people who, over the years, have refused to change their ways or accept the advantages of civilization. One might well ask, "Have our missionaries labored and sacrificed in vain?"

Most assuredly not. Hundreds have left the "devil grounds" to join coastal villages where their children attend Adventist schools and become baptized members of the church. An example is Pastor Dick, whose mother was murdered by his Big Nambus father. From this background he has become a stalwart who served several years as missionary in New Guinea, and now he works for his people in the New Hebrides.

I saw schools and churches everywhere, and saw hundreds of bright young people who have no further interest in the devil-worshiping rituals of the jungle villages, for the faithful witness of our missionaries over the years is ripening to a rich harvest. The devil's citadel cannot forever withstand the onslaught of the Gospel of love.

STRANGE DEVIL DOINGS

It was a year later when Pastors R. W. Taylor, Dean Giles, and Leo Rose, with Dr. Joeli, made another trip into the center of Malekula. Taylor described the visit.

> A couple of hundred yards along the track from Makauwe we saw on the right a clump of bamboo surrounding a pit. I knew that this was the place where the witch doctor talks to the evil spirits. When he desires to commune with the spirits, he comes to this place and takes a bamboo passing it through a loosely woven bamboo fence and over the pit. Now the priest begins to sing a song inviting the arrival of the devil, and before long he begins to feel someone take hold of the end of the bamboo and pull him in through the fence to the enclosure. The villagers told me that even though all the men in the village tried to hold on to the witch doctor, this was impossible, as a power stronger than them all dragged the man forward into the enclosure; whereupon the evil priest became possessed and began to speak the word of the devil, foretelling disaster to befall the tribe and also indicate where certain lost articles might be found, beside other communications.
>
> Passing a house, we noticed some skulls through the rotted thatch—gruesome decorations. Suddenly a head appeared from the small door opening in one of the men's houses, a gaunt but smiling face protruded, and I heard the words spoken to Doctor Joeli: "Me feller glad now you come along village. Me feller gotten plenty sick." Immediately Doctor Joeli was busy with his bag of medicines and his stethoscope. I was interested to discover that no matter what else he prescribed the first part of the treatment was, "You go to river and you washim good." To these people who seem not to wash the whole of their lives, this must indeed have seemed like a treatment.

DRUMS AND DRUM MUSIC

> The people of this area are expert drum makers, using large logs up to eight or nine feet long, which they carve with the features of a human being at the top and then through a very narrow opening down the length of the log, they carve out the interior of these hardwood tree trunks. When all is completed, the logs are stood on end and placed in a hole in the ground and remain in this upright position. The largest of the drums is called the mother drum, and Makauwe had just erected a new mother drum which

was surrounded by four other smaller drums. Additionally they have a number of smaller hollowed logs which are left lying on the ground and are beaten with sticks much like a kettle drum.

I brought my tape recorder with the idea of recording this rather unique sound. Each drum has its own note and as they play together each one takes its turn playing a solo part. We found the Big Nambus men very cooperative in providing the drum music, and an excellent recording was obtained. We discovered that there were different kinds of beats for different occasions, and I asked what was the significance of the particular beat which I had just recorded. We were told that this was the beat for the pig-killing ceremony, associated with their sacrifices to their heathen gods. As each solo drum played its part the chief was to kill a pig and then as the other drums joined in, he was to cut it up and then the drums went softer, and once more as the new soloist played his part it was time to kill another pig. As these ceremonies involved forty or fifty, or even a hundred or more pigs, the drummer must have been kept busy for a long time as they provided the rhythm for this background of death.

Nearby the women were still wearing their typical Nambus headgear made of a number of layers of grass, while their only other covering was a much smaller loincloth of the same grass. Some of our Adventist girls had come with us to assist the doctor, and as we compared our Christian girls with the village girls of the same Nambus stock, the contrast was overwhelming.

BIG NAMBUS BREAKTHROUGH

For fifty-five years the gospel pounded at the citadel of the Nambus cannibals. When at last, in 1969, there was a visible crack in the wall of heathenism, missionaries were elated. W. J. Paynter, of the New Hebrides Mission, reported,

> Malekula was the first challenge to the early missionaries as they made their first permanent homes on the little island of Atchin, a safe distance off the coast of Malekula. The dark mountains of Malekula were like gauntlets thrown down before their faces, for they knew that they concealed unknown numbers of men who had never heard the good news of the Gospel of peace and salvation for all men. Yet, as the years went on, they seemed to have a definite resistance to the advance of Christianity.
>
> But today it is thrilling to see a change taking place. We have tried our best for years to make friends with the chief of the Amok in the center

of the Big Nambus area. We have visited him, talked with him, given clothing to his people, given medical service, offered to put a teacher in his village if he wished it, but for years the negative response was like a stone wall. He has always been friendly, but distant. In recent years the pace has quickened as the government officer has tried various means to be allowed to send a teacher and put a school among these people. Other mission bodies also have made special appeals in order to get a worker into this, one of the last strongholds of heathenism. But the chief's reaction has been firmly negative. This has gone on for years, and everybody realized it was not just lack of action on the chief's part, but positive resistance to the pressures of our civilization.

Late last year the chief weakened, and half-promised to allow the government to put a teacher in the area. When our pastor visited him shortly thereafter, he mentioned what he had told the district officer, who looked at our pastor and said he would let him know more later. Sure enough, at the time of our next contact, several months later, the chief told us he had not allowed the government to put in a teacher—but he said no more than that. It was some months after that a deputation from Amok journeyed down from the mountains to our school on the coast, bringing a request from the chief that two of his boys be allowed to come to our school this year.

Could they? Why of course they could! "Bring them down just as soon as you like." These two boys are now students in our church school at Tanmaru right now. Despite their heathen background and their complete lack of schooling, so far they have fit in quite well, and are very happy.

It is a wonderful breakthrough to have these boys in our school, for it is more than having just two more boys there as students. The fact that they were put there by the chief of the Amok, means that this is the beginning of a different attitude on the part of these people of the Amok Nambus area towards civilization and education. It is a good indication that we have gained their confidence more than others, and that associations with them in the future should grow closer and we should be able to help them spiritually. It means that this center of heathenism is weakening for a collapse into a Christian way of life. Now we are praying hopefully that this is the opening of the door for which we have been waiting for over fifty years. The infamous Big Nambus people may yet prove to be stalwart soldiers for Christ.

The Tanmaru school, located at the place where Norman Wiles was buried, was itself an answer to prayer. It was made possible largely by funds raised by the local people and donations. It was planned as a two-teacher

school with four elementary grades, though there were misgivings at the time. But the new concrete building became a reality, and in the first year in operation it was bulging with pupils. Now if God adds the heathen of the Amok area to our interest, the numbers will swell considerably. But we like that kind of a headache, and ask you to pray with us that this may be the opening for these darkened people to know the true God.

CHAPTER 19

STEPPING HOPEFULLY INTO THE SEVENTIES

On May 5, 1970, over three hundred people climbed the hill to the grave of Norman Wiles on the fiftieth anniversary of his death. A special service at his graveside at Tanmaru recalled his sacrifice and the faithful witness of other pioneer missionaries and national workers.

In 1920 there were no Seventh-day Adventist churches, schools, or members in this area. That day saw a young woman bury her husband alone and reluctantly leave the mission station. That day saw sorrow and apparent defeat, but God's Word does not return unto Him void. "He that goeth forth and weepeth, bearing precious seed, shall doubtless come again with rejoicing, bringing his sheaves with him" (Psalm 126:6).

Now the picture of Tanmaru, and indeed in all the New Hebrides, has changed since that sad day. Half a mile from the grave a school of sixty children, and other schools and churches within a few miles, are fruitage of the gospel among these Big Nambus people. The fine building at Tanmaru was erected with funds sent to the New Hebrides by Alma Wiles, who then lived in California, USA. The picture is a continual reminder to the local people of service prompted by true dedication to Christ.

ARE FOREIGN MISSIONS WORTH THE EFFORT?

This question has been asked before, and it is a valid one worth considering. In 1973, Dr. John F. Knight with five other laymen from the Epping Adventist Church, Sydney, Australia, were so pressed for an answer, they went out to

see for themselves. As Knight said, "It was a self-designed, self-sponsored trip aimed at discovering lots of answers to perennial questions."

The New Hebrides was chosen because this church had a particular interest in Parker Missionary College, located on the island of Aore, just off the southern coast of Santo. "What does a mission station really look like?" they asked. "Are the pictures and stories anything like the reality? Are missions in foreign lands really worthwhile?" These were some of the questions that prompted the visit. After his trip, Dr. Knight reported,

> "You want to keep away from that place," our pilot said, thrusting a thumb in the direction of a vast expanse of green below. "Malekula Island. The Big Nambus live there. Wildest mob on earth. Still eat humans, it is said." After uttering these reassuring words, the pilot stared straight ahead again, guiding our little nine-seater Melanesian Airways plane towards Santo airstrip.
>
> The New Hebrides consists of a mass of islands extending in a north-south line. The capital, Port Vila, is rising to fame as the latest tax haven. The intense interest in this picturesque but backwater island town is evidenced by the skyrocketing land prices. To pay $20,000 to $30,000 for single house blocks is commonplace. Santo is roughly 300 miles to the north of Port Vila, this capital being on the island of Efate, with the celebrated, and still fierce, Malekula Island between. Santo is an even more remote backwater. The entire business center is made up of one main street, no hotel (their one and only was burned down a few months ago), a collection of dilapidated shops, plus a well-constructed Burns Philip emporium.
>
> One of the neatest structures there is the New Hebrides Mission headquarters of the Seventh-day Adventist Church. Here we met Pastor Eric Winter, President, and John Allum, Secretary-treasurer. Meeting these happy people in such a remote frontier was exhilarating. But our final destination was the Parker Missionary College on another island, negotiable only by mission launch.

PARKER MISSION

Rani II, the mission launch, is packed with freight every time it makes the trip from Santo to Parker. This twenty-foot stoic of a ship seems less than minute as it bobs along in the wide-open Pacific, laden with goods. From the college a magnificent beach fronts onto the Pacific Ocean. Closely cropped lawns run up from the sea and merge into the college buildings. Further

back this again merges into a wilderness of green coconut palms, heavy tropical bush, and dense foliage. It didn't take very long to discover that this mission is more than a single enterprise. It is virtually divided into a variety of departments: general education, spiritual education, money-raising projects, general maintenance and rebuilding projects, and hospital and medical care.

At present about 150 New Hebrideans are receiving an education. The age spectrum is wide. The youngest are [in the] twelve-to-fourteen-year age bracket, and the oldest from twenty to thirty years of age. In due course these will become teachers in their own right. Some will go out to villages where "calls" are being made for teachers, and will establish church spearheads in these places. Classes occupy the entire morning and the bells shatter the peaceful atmosphere at strident intervals. As only the bellboy has a clock, all must pay attention to the sound of the bell. The classrooms are substandard by European standards. But we were assured, they are quite reasonable by local standards, and we discovered this to be true.

In many cases, current native students are barely one generation removed from savagery. Their normal standard of living would give a white man nightmares, but to the native people it represents an escalation of values. Tuition costs about $70 a year, and each student must find this amount before he comes to college. With the high price of copra, until recently, this has been easy to come by. Many could readily earn these fees during the year-end vacation. In people who have just recently emerged from heathenism the capacity for learning does not seem to be high. Indeed their capability for doing many things that come natural to us seems very limited. One wonders with trepidation, what will be the outcome of moves for self-rule among the people in these areas. Nearly every white man located here holds the same fears. Nevertheless, as the days of the white man are definitely numbered in most of these islands, the need for [educating] the native people becomes even more urgent if the Gospel ministry hopes to survive.

THE SPIRITUAL SIDE

The Seventh-day Adventist Church is the only remaining body operating an independent educational and medical work in the New Hebrides. These islands used to be a stronghold of the Presbyterian Church. But the Presbyterians have thrown in their lot with the government, seeming

content to pass the responsibilities of these departments over to state control. As with any church-run college, spiritual education at Parker Missionary College receives considerable attention. There is a sense of spirituality in the atmosphere. Soon after the rising bell early in the morning, the delightful harmony of gospel songs drifts through the tropical atmosphere as the students prepare for meals and classes, all unrehearsed and unscheduled. Everyone comes to church meetings. It may be that there is nothing else to do, and it represents the spiritual cum-social event of the day. The well-constructed timber church is practically filled to capacity. The part singing of the students is truly beautiful. They seem to have a natural talent for singing. Their energetic voices lifted in praise stir the heart as nothing else can. Nobody trains them; there is no accompaniment. They sing because they are happy, and this comes through loud and clear. Pastor Sam Dick looks after the meetings. He is a quiet, unobtrusive character, but his background is not so disarming. He has seen bitter days of warfare and bloodshed, was brought up in the cannibal days of the Big Nambus on Malekula, had a simple conversion and wonderful transformation, and now leads the Parker students.

Right now Parker College is facing a real problem, as are dozens of plantation owners, because of the discovery of a synthetic substitute found for copra. It used to be $200 a ton, and it dropped to $30 per ton. Owners are going wild. Coconuts lie by the millions where they fall. In many parts the jungle is again taking over. The mission budget is suddenly down $4,000. Plus, it has 150 students to employ each afternoon in other activities. But the battle is not all lost. The college has developed the only dairy herd in the New Hebrides. About sixty cows have been rounded up from stray herds running wild on the island. From these an excellent dairy industry has been established with modern milking machines. So each morning many gallons of milk are shipped to Burns Philip on Santo, where it finds a ready sale, and here there is scope for future production, transported by our own little vessel, *Rani II*.

THE AORE HOSPITAL

Dr. Knight continued,

A short distance from the training school lies the Aore Hospital. This is a delightful rural-type hospital, much the same as you would find out West in

Australia. It has eighteen beds and is full most of the time. It is run by Dr. Joeli, a dedicated native of Fiji who went through the Fiji Medical School about twelve years ago. His name is well known throughout the New Hebrides and is indeed an example of true Christianity. He carries out his duties with scholarly dignity. He converses in good English, and will escort visitors around his domain with obvious pride. He is a long way from his colleagues out here and loves discussing cases with visiting physicians.

RADIO SERVICE

Apart from those who attend personally, there is also radio diagnosing and treating. Twice daily, at twelve noon and 6:00 p.m., the mission has a half hour. Often a distant worker will give details of an acutely ill person, and seek assistance of Dr. Joeli. Listening to this two-way conversation on these radio sessions must be the eighth wonder of the world, but it seems to work. Patients are treated where they are, many miles removed in some unreachable spot, or else they may decide to send the mission vessel to bring them the hospital. This really brings help to those who need it most.

Our stay at Parker was all too short. As *Rani II*, carrying us with the cans of milk from the dairy, pulled out from the tiny wharf, we waved farewell to our mission friends. It was 5:00 a.m. and just getting light. The streaks of dawn silhouetted the coconut palms in a quiet, unforgettable beauty.

A BIG, BIG HEART

Since our return, our friends have asked, "What did you think of the mission field?" "Do you think missions are worth all the effort?" Of course the answer lies in one's point of view. To begin with, I've developed a new view of the people who leave the homeland and head for these far-flung primitive places. The problems they have to face—the difficulties, disadvantages and disasters are never-ending. It requires a stoic heart, a big, big heart. It calls for great fortitude, an indomitable courage that not many people possess. Mission fields are not for the weak. You must be physically robust and mentally agile.

You must be prepared to live with adversity as your daily companion, to accept difficulties over which you have no control, as part of the deal. You

must have an inbuilt faith that what you are doing is God's command to you. An on-the-spot visit indicates that any upgrading of human beings from the dregs of heathenism is worthwhile. The transformation must be seen to be believed. The pictures on the Appeal magazines are genuine and the stories they tell are authentic. It is our firm belief, gained at firsthand from a layman's visit to, and appraisal of, the mission field, that they warrant the continued support of every member of the Christian Church. The funds you subscribe are used to the maximum. They are necessary. They are fulfilling an urgent need in obeying the Divine Commission, which is to give the Gospel "to every nation, kindred, tongue and people."

"WHAT HATH GOD WROUGHT!"

"To very few come the opportunity to draw the contrast between conditions as they are now and as they were four decades ago," said Pastor A. G. Stewart, after a return visit to the New Hebrides in 1958, forty years after.

No place in the New Hebrides affords a better example of the change than the islands of Atchin and Malekula. On our arrival the superintendent of police told us, "Atchin has the worst people of all! If you can make any impression on them in twenty years you will be doing well!"

On Atchin the 600 people that inhabited this small island were cannibals, still stalking their fellowmen. They were all illiterate, living in low, damp, dark houses frequently used as stables for high-priced and coveted tusked boars. In semi-nude condition, dirty and foul-smelling through the constant use of dark tobacco, they were also diseased by the use of swine's flesh and unclean creatures from the sea. Almost all the children suffered from yaws.

Victims to the slavery of heathen traditions and ceremonies, they were goaded on year in and year out by the whims and dictates of the so-called departed spirits who kept them in a constant state of fear. Not a yard of ordinary wearing apparel could be seen anywhere, but the women wore a small piece of plaited mats around their hips, and the men wore less. The women were in a state of suppression as the servants of those who had bought them as wives for so many pigs. Even girls of tender years were betrothed to men old enough to be their fathers or grandfathers. When finally dragged to the compound or enclosure owned by their purchaser, the girls were subjected to leg-burning as punishment if they refused to stay. Much of the time was spent in feasting and dancing, and often licentious

gratification, leaving them so debauched and degraded that they did not recover for several days.

Need you wonder that following three years of patient endeavor by my predecessor, Pastor Parker, I spent some six years of prayerful and almost constant effort before baptizing the first group of converts. Now, looking back over forty years, I would that all critics of the real worth of missionary service among a one-time degraded people could have seen and heard what we have during the last few weeks in mission stations of the New Hebrides.

As we approached the foreshore of the island of Atchin we were greeted by at least 100 of those happy people: sturdy men bringing to the boat an improvised chair-like raft upon which Mrs. Stewart, Pastor McCutcheon and I were soon seated and carried right to the door of a large new church completed about a year ago, the workmanship of Atchin young men. The members had donated about 4,000 pounds (then $16,000) to purchase the material. This church has seating for 300—half the island's population.

The older and much smaller church that I built forty years ago, with the help of a few lads, still stands nearby in a state of fair preservation. It is used for a school, and on Sabbath for junior Sabbath School. A brief walk across the island revealed a marked change. The compound on which stood heathen huts and pig sties is now used as garden groves, while the old heathen drums are in a state of decay. Surely a new song is being sung in the isles. To those who once sat in the region of the shadow of death, light is sprung up.

In the evening, as the sun was setting, we assembled to greet the Sabbath. We leave it to your imagination to picture the scene as we took our places on the rostrum in this large new church, well ventilated, kept spotless, and filled to capacity with people redeemed from heathen darkness, faces shining, singing from their hearts the good old advent hymns. Recalling with difficulty the language I acquired forty years ago, language that was unwritten, I spoke to a reverent, attentive audience on the promise of Christ to His disciples: "I will come again." The following morning, the climax of our visit was reached as the conclusion of another such message. The response was spontaneous. Hearts were full, as with trembling voices and tears of joy men and women who were boys and girls in our first school, but now fathers and mothers, pledged again their devotion to God.

The scene was unforgettable, and with the Master I say again, "Blessed are your eyes for they see, and your ears for they hear those things which ye hear." "They that sow in tears shall reap in joy. He that goeth forth and weepeth bearing precious seed shall doubtless come again with rejoicing, bringing his sheaves with him."

Today, infamous Malekula with its murky past, is studded with jewels and precious stones mined from the deep recesses of heathenism where some tribes are still untamed. Many leave their pagan mountain haunts and join the Christian villages along the coast. It is a risky breakaway, but they find a new life and the transforming power of the gospel. Malekula has been branded as the darkest island of the Pacific, yet our latest report shows 500 baptized into Christ and the Seventh-day Adventist Church. There are ten of these organized churches and a flourishing school at Tanmaru with three teachers. Besides there are many unbaptized adherents who regularly attend worship and mission activities but as yet are uncounted.

The Malekula figures were supplied by Pastor Sam Dick, once leader of missions on Malekula, now on the school faculty at Aore. (He is the same Sam Dick whose story is related in chapter 1, whose father killed his mother when the pig got loose.) Other islands were more responsive to the gospel; none was more difficult than Malekula. As for the New Hebrides island group, the everlasting gospel has been gathering momentum over the decades. Now, as reported in 1979, there are 4,101 baptized members, 34 churches, 20 elementary schools with 1,014 pupils, a secondary training school with an enrollment of 152, and mission workers, including ordained ministers and teachers of 85.

So we bid farewell to the man-eaters of Malekula. In recognition of a combined effort of the human and Divine, we exclaim, "What hath God wrought!"

APPENDIX I

THE NEW HEBRIDES BECOME AN INDEPENDENT NATION

Britain and France gave up their seventy-four-year joint rule of the New Hebrides archipelago on July 30, 1980. The two nations' flags were lowered in separate ceremonies in Port Vila, the capital, on the island of Efate, at midnight on July 29, and the Reverend Walter Lini, an Anglican priest, was sworn in as the first prime minister of the new nation of Vanuatu.

As the time approached for independence, several parties had competed for the right to rule this new nation. There was the Vanuaaku Pati led by Father Lini, the Namakl Movement, the Tabwemasana, and the Federal Party of the New Hebrides, one branch of which was the Nagriamel, led by Jimmy (Moli) Stevens. The election was held November 14, 1979, nine months before Independence Day, and observers were appointed by the United Nations secretary-general, who visited the island group from November 11 to 19. There were representatives from Australia, Fiji, Ivory Coast, and the Republic of the Cameroon. They declared the elections to be fair, free, according to the electoral regulations, and reflecting the will of the people. Lini's Vanaaku Pati won easily and was given the right to govern. There was celebration on the one hand and disappointment on the other.

Jimmy Stevens, a bearded, patriarchal-looking Scotchman and a former bulldozer operator, did not relish his defeat, nor would he comply with election results. He argued with the United Nations' representatives that the people at large did not understand the elections, particularly the bush people, and that the island natives would not be ready for a democratic government for ten to fifteen

years. The group needed a strong power for protection. Besides, he said, the amalgamation of these islands into one nation was merely the colonial powers' arrangement without the consent of individual islands. So why could not one island like Santo declare itself independent if the population wanted it?

Mr. Stevens had the support of a questionable group of locals—French sympathizers, some Christians, animists, cargo cultists, and a sect that worshiped Prince Philip as a god. Some of his financial backing came from the United States, where the Phoenix Foundation of Nevada was looking for an independent island as a tax haven; where there would be little government regulation and no taxes, a free and easy paradise where anyone could come and go at will, promote trade, develop industry, quietly attend to his own plantation, or ignore responsibility and live on yams and other island products that require minimum effort for tropical living.

This hopeful leader gathered to himself a ragtag army and mounted a rebellion. Clad in loincloths and plastic helmets, these soldiers armed with bows and arrows, machetes, ancient muskets, and clubs stormed some old World War II army huts, overran the business area, and looted shops of tons of food, then wrecked private homes and carried off furniture. Some Adventist national workers lost their homes this way. Then Jimmy Stevens took the British commissioner as a hostage, commandeered the radio station, and declared himself absolute ruler, proceeding immediately to exercise his powers.

All British residents were commanded to leave Santo, so Adventist pastor Bill Townend and his associates left for Aore. The rebellion affected the work of our mission leadership for six months, after which the property was restored and workers returned. During the rebellion, however, there was considerable chaos on Santo as the bow-and-arrow army raided homes, shops, and hotels. Tourists lost their belongings, shops their stock, and homes their furniture.

The British and French argued over who was to blame and how to meet the crisis. Oliver Stern, French minister of foreign affairs, said that they would guarantee the safety of the people but would not resort to military intervention after independence.

Finally the two powers sent in two Hercules C-130 transports loaded with 250 British marines and French paratroopers, plus three helicopters. If they expected to meet musket-busters, a shower of arrows, or some formidable force of club-wielding cults, they were disappointed. Armed for deadly combat, they were greeted with garlands of roses as a thousand islanders curiously watched the friendly confrontation—the finest war in recent times. The commissioner was released, the bow-and-arrow war petered out, and Jimmy Stevens was awarded fourteen years in prison, while the Reverend Father Lini tries his hand at being prime minister.

APPENDIX II

IMPORTANT FACTS ABOUT THE NEW HEBRIDES—NOW VANUATU

This territory consists of a Y-shaped chain of some eighty islands, 400 miles from north to south. These islands lie about 2,000 miles east of Sydney, Australia, and 500 miles west of Fiji.

Population: 112,596 in 1979; 273,307 in 2016.

Gross National Product (per capita): US$540 in 1978; US$5,730 in 2016

Rainfall: 90 inches per year, on average.

Government: The group was administered jointly by the British and French, Condominium Government, for 74 years (October 1906 to July 1980). British and French flags flew side by side. High commissioners represented each country. In 1975 general elections took place to elect a representative assembly to replace the former advisory council. Further elections were held in 1979. The assembly chose its own president and full independence was set for July 30, 1980.

Planning and Economy: The Planning Development Office was taken over by the Chief Minister's Office in 1978, which was to chart the transition to independence. Finances for the plan were sought equally from France, the United Kingdom, and Australia. Assistance was also provided for by multilateral agencies

such as the European Development Fund or United National Development Fund. New Zealand and Canada also provided aid. The plan envisioned an expenditure for takeover and development activities of AUD$31,932,000.

Production: The main commercial crops are copra, cocoa, and coffee. Yams, taro, manioc, and bananas are grown for local consumption. A large number of cattle are reared on plantations, also goats, pigs, and poultry. A manganese mine on Efate contributes to exports. There is also a sawmill, a soft-drink factory, and a fish-freezing plant. This freezing plant is on Santo and exports to Japan and elsewhere. There are no heavy industries. Australia and France were reported to be the major sources of imports, which are machinery, transport equipment, foodstuffs, manufactured goods, and mineral fuels.

Roads: The Public Works Department maintains limited roads on Efate, Santo, Tanna, Pentecost, Aoba, Ambrym, and Malekula. These are in addition to usable dirt roads for motor vehicles.

Airways: External air services are provided by Air Pacific, Unions de Transports Aeriens, Solomon Islands Airways, and Air Nauru. Air Pacific has two services a week to Nandi-Villa-Honiara-Brisbane, besides a number of other services. Inter-island flights are provided by Air Melanesia. The principal airports are Baur Field for Port Vila, and Pekoa for Santo. Seventeen airports provide an internal network.

Shipping: Several international shipping lines serve the group, linking the country with Australia, New Zealand, and other Pacific territories, notably Hong Kong, Japan, America, and Europe. Small vessels provide inter-island service.

Telecommunications: Internal telephone and telegraph services are provided by Posts and Telecommunications and Radio departments. There are automatic telephone exchanges at Port Vila and Santo. External telegraph, telephone, and telex services are provided through Hebrite through their satellite earth station at Port Vila. Radio New Hebrides broadcasts seven days a week in three languages: English, French, and pidgin.

Languages: There are over a hundred local languages in 2016. Bislama is spoken by 33.7 percent of the population, while English and French only account for 2 percent and 0.6 percent respectively.

Education: Under the Condominium Government, education was the responsibility of both the British and French national services, which organized parallel and separate systems. Each made a subsidy to its administration for education purposes. Grant aid was given to four education committees with 112 primary schools and to the Diocese of the New Hebrides with 22 primary schools. There were many mission schools of varying standards. There were 112 students sponsored by the British National Services studying overseas. Literacy in 2016 is 85.25 percent for adults over 15 years of age. Youth literacy is 95.74 percent for ages 15–24 years.

Health: Medical care is provided through a network of 106 hospitals, health centers, clinics, and dispensaries administered by the combined medical department with the help of a number of voluntary agencies, including mission bodies. Malaria is still the most serious of the major endemic diseases, which also include tuberculosis, leprosy filariasis, and venereal disease. Life expectancy in 2016 is 63 years for males and 66.4 years for females.

Religion: In 2016, 70 percent of the population is Protestant. Of this, 12.5 percent are Seventh-day Adventists. Vanuatu is part of the South Pacific Division, the Trans Pacific Union Mission, and the Vanuatu Mission of Seventh-day Adventists. Seventh-day Adventist Church membership in 2014 was 21,354. There were 85 organized churches, 130 companies, 6 medical clinics and dispensaries, and 64 teachers and licensed or ordained ministers. There is a secondary school, Aore Adventist Academy.

APPENDIX III

ALMA BERNICE WILES

Alma Bernice Butz was born in Benicia, California, on September 23, 1894. Her parents were Edwin Sebastian Butz and Florence M. Davis. Edwin's father was German and his mother was from Ohio, USA. He was born in Illinois in 1865. Florence was from Iowa, born in 1868. They married on June 2, 1892, in the Napa Valley of California.

In 1895, when Alma was just eight months old, they were asked to go as missionaries to the island of Pitcairn. They were there one year and then moved to Tonga. In 1901, they attended the General Conference session that was held in Battle Creek, Michigan, where Edwin Butz was ordained. They returned to Tonga and then in 1906 moved to Australia, where Pastor Butz became the president of the South Australian Conference. It was here that Alma grew up.

One day she answered the door to find a young man, Norman Wiles, with a message from his mother to her father. They became friends, and when Norman left for Australasian Missionary College in 1911, Alma was not far behind. At the end of 1914, Norman graduated and was appointed to be a missionary in the New Hebrides (now Vanuatu). He and Alma were married on December 24, 1914, in Brisbane, Queensland, as her father was now president of the Queensland Conference. They then went to the Sydney Sanitarium to take a course in tropical medicine. In 1915 they sailed to the Island of Atchin, in the New Hebrides, to prepare for their work on Malekula.

After several weeks they were taken to the northwest side of the island, where

the people had never before seen a white woman. Some of the tribes were cannibals, particularly the Big Nambus, who lived in the mountains. It was very difficult adapting to life on Malekula. Malaria was prevalent, and more than once they had to return to Australia to regain their health and strength in order to carry on. But some of the young men became friendly, and even the Big Nambus allowed Norman to visit and tell stories of Jesus from the Sabbath School picture rolls.

After five years, one Sabbath morning Norman had a meeting arranged with the Big Nambus, but he was coming down with malaria and Alma urged him not to go. However, he felt he should go. By the time he got home he was very sick. They realized it was the dreaded blackwater fever. For five days Alma nursed him without relief. She had asked a young man to go for help but found out later that he did not go. On May 5, 1920, Norman died. He was not yet twenty-eight years old.

Alma was able to get some help in digging his grave but had to bury him at night and make sure it was well hidden. Then she escaped through the jungle along the coast and eventually made her way to the island of Atchin, where she collapsed in the arms of the missionaries there. It was July before she was able to get a boat to take her back to Australia. Her mother met her and took her to the sanitarium, and they stayed there until she regained her health. At this time her father was preceptor and Bible teacher at the college.

Alma wished to go back to the New Hebrides, but the brethren advised her to first get her nursing degree. So in 1922 she returned to America. She studied at the College of Medical Evangelists and the White Memorial Hospital in California. On September 5, 1925, she received her registered nurse certificate. On June 16, 1926, the California State Board of Health granted her the RN diploma. She then proceeded to Michigan, where at Emmanuel Missionary College she studied library courses and received her bachelor of arts degree on May 22, 1928.

Meanwhile back in Australia, her sister-in-law, Vida Emma Wiles, was married on February 1, 1927, to Edward (Ted) Charles Harris. Their daughter, Zelma Beryl (this writer) was born on January 31, 1928, followed by their son Roy Norman, who was born April 13, 1929. Alma's parents had now retired and visited the island of Pitcairn for the first time in thirty-four years. They later returned and settled in the city of Melbourne, Victoria. Alma visited them and also her Wiles in-laws.

She applied to go to Papua, New Guinea, and was sent to Aroma in 1934. She practiced nursing and cared for mission posts while the missionaries were on furlough, such as the Mitchells at Viliarupu and others at Bisiatabu. Her

work was mainly with women, and she saved hundreds of lives—mothers and their babies. She taught the women how to cook healthy food, take care of their babies, and sew dresses.

During one of her furlough trips it was planned that I would travel to Papua, New Guinea, when I was 15 years old and spend several months with her in Aroma. But in 1941, Japan bombed Pearl Harbor, Hawaii, and the Pacific became embroiled in World War II. As Japan took over island groups in the Coral Sea, missionaries had to be evacuated to Australia. Alma came back and stayed with her parents but worked with the conferences in keeping the mission work before the church members.

In the summer of 1947, Roy (my brother) and I, with two friends, took a road trip and arrived at Avondale when a missionary conference was being held. Alma was there, and as she was anxious for me to attend Avondale, she took me to see the principal, Dr. W. G. C. Murdoch, who offered to write to my father. The result was that when college started in 1948, I was a student there. By the time it was safe for the women to return to Papua, New Guinea, Pastor and Mrs. Butz were in their 80s and Alma had decided to stay and care for them. Pastor Butz died in 1956 and Mrs. Butz in 1957.

After the deaths of her parents, Alma returned to America and took refresher nursing courses, receiving her RN from the Maryland State Board in August of 1959, and from California in October of 1959. On November 10, 1959, she went to Nigeria, to the Adventist-owned Ile-Ife Hospital, and was head of the midwifery department, teaching the nurses there midwifery. At the age of sixty-seven she had to return to America because she had developed diabetes. She hoped to return to Nigeria, but she was not allowed to do so. Instead, she returned to Australia, and on May 22, 1963, she took my mother, Vida Harris, to the New Hebrides. It was her first time back since Norman's death in 1920. They received a wonderful welcome and found that the people of the northwestern coast of Malekula were all Seventh-day Adventists. One old man remembered them as he was just a child when she and Norman worked there. Alma and my mother visited with Dr. Joeli at Aore Hospital and were asked to view the birth of a little girl. The mother then asked my mother to name the baby. Since my daughter and Vida's granddaughter was just five years old, Mother named the baby Janelle. Somewhere in Vanuatu there is a 52-year-old woman named Janelle. How we would love to meet her.

In December of 1963, my family drove from Queensland to Western Australia to take up a conference appointment. When we passed through Melbourne, we stayed with Auntie Alma for a weekend. Shortly after that she sold her parents' home and returned to America. For a time, she lived in Portland, Oregon,

and then she moved down to California. Her health demanded that she move into the Rialto Nursing Home, which is near Loma Linda. A few months before her death, I was able to visit with her for a whole week. She died on March 23, 1980, and is buried in the Montecito Cemetery. A service was held in Loma Linda, and then another memorial service at the Glendale City Church, for she had worked at the Glendale Hospital several times.

Zelma Beryl Harris Edwards
May 10, 2015

APPENDIX IV

NAOMI

There is one more chapter that needs to be added to this story. Andrew Stewart tells about when he first came to Atchin and met the Wiles family, who had come to the neighboring island to welcome them. Mrs. Stewart had heard that Alma had been taking care of a native baby girl who was rescued from being buried with her mother. Jean Stewart noticed there was no baby with them and asked about it.

"Oh, don't mention it," pleaded Alma. "It's too sad for words. We had her for two months, and she was doing so beautifully that we were simply overjoyed. Then the father, who had been willing to have her buried alive, had a change of heart. He heard of the progress she was making and the interest she was creating, and apparently he thought he should be getting the glory. So he marched to our house and, with a note of authority, demanded her return. We all protested hotly and pleaded that she be allowed to stay a little longer before he took her back. But to no avail. He became angry and shouted, 'Piccaninni belong me, e no belong you,' and with that he took the little thing from us and returned her to the filthy hut and to the company of pigs, bugs, and starvation."

Norman and Alma were never allowed to see the baby again despite their best attempts. Andrew and Jean Stewart felt that, as newcomers, maybe they could make better progress. After a few inquiries they found out a hut did exist with a girl Piccaninni. "No, the baby didn't have a mother. And yes, she had once been with a missionary."

The hut was located, and there on a banana leaf lay the tiny brown baby,

emaciated and dirty. They turned to find a large native man looking at them. Jean had tears in her eyes. He spoke more gently, "Missus like look out along this Piccaninni?"

"Indeed I would," Jean hastened to say, "but her papa won't let her come back along mission."

"Oh?" questioned he with a lofty air. "Me chief along this place. Nale, name belong me. Me can talk along papa belong 'im. You go back along house. By and by Piccaninni he come. Some fella mary 'e can take 'im."

Sure enough, later that evening there was a knock at the door, and a native woman delivered the tiny infant to Jean. She promptly gave the baby a bath and fixed a bottle of milk. The girl didn't look like she would survive the night, but with feedings every two hours, she began to thrive.

The Stewarts raised Naomi as their own. They took her to conference sessions with them. And when they left the country to attend General Conference, they enrolled her in a school on Fiji. She developed beautifully in her Christian education, and as a lovely young woman.

Pastor Stewart tells of another miracle in Naomi's story.

> I had returned to my post (in Atchin) and preached one Sabbath in our home station in the language we had laboriously mastered. I felt impelled to make an urgent appeal at the close of my service. So repeating the words of my text, I called on the listeners, "If any man thirst, let him come unto Me and drink."
>
> "Don't hesitate. Come now." Among those who responded was one from whom I could hardly take my eyes. It was Naomi's father.
>
> He wanted to speak, and this is what he said, "Today, I cut my last tie with heathenism. You, Pastor Stewart, have been building a house on this island with saplings [young people]; but today I promise to give my heart to God and become a corner post in this church. I thank Mrs. Stewart for caring for my child; and tell Naomi that if I do not see her again in this life, I promise to meet her in heaven."

When Naomi's father was baptized, he changed his name to Pana and became a strong influence in the church.

In 1936 Naomi was married to Mosese Magese, a keen, clear-eyed Fijian. Pastor Stewart married them after Mrs. Stewart gave her away. Soon they became parents to a baby boy, whom they named Andrew Graham Stewart. Sadly, Naomi died two years later. Her boy, Andrew, grew up to be a teacher and educational secretary in the New Hebrides. He married Susan, and they had three daughters.

BIBLIOGRAPHY

Australasian Record. Warburton, Victoria, Australia: Australasian Division of the Seventh-day Adventist Church, 1912–1981.

Barnard, Marjorie. *A History of Australia*, reprint ed. New York: Frederick Praeger, 1964.

Encyclopædia Britannica. Chicago: Encyclopædia Britannica, 2010.

Falcone, James W. *John Geddie, Hero of the New Hebrides*. Toronto: Presbyterian Press, 1915.

Herndon, Booton. *The 7th Day*. Washington, DC: Review and Herald®, 1963. First published 1960 by McGraw Hill.

Margull, H. J. *The Bible in the World*. World Council of Churches, 1965.

Matthews, Basil. *John Williams the Ship Builder*. London: Oxford University Press, 1915.

Miller, J. Graham. *Live: A History of Church Planting in the New Hebrides to 1880*. Vol. 1. Sydney, Australia: Presbyterian Church of Australia, [1978].

Morrell, W. P. *Britain in the Pacific Islands*. Oxford: Clarendon Press, 1960.

Neil, Stephen. *A History of Christian Missions*. Grand Rapids, MI: Eerdmans, 1965.

Olsen, M. Ellsworth. *Origins and Progress of Seventh-day Adventists*. Washing-

ton, DC: Review and Herald®, 1926.

Paton, John G. *John G. Paton: An Autobiography*. James Paton, ed. 12th ed. London: Banner of Truth Trust, 1965.

Paxton, John, ed. *The Statesman's Yearbook*. New York: St. Martin's Press.

Seventh-day Adventist Church Yearbook 2016. Silver Spring, MD: Office of Archives, Statistics, and Research of the General Conference of Seventh-day Adventists, 2016.

Seventh-day Adventist Encyclopedia. 2nd revised ed. Hagerstown, MD: Review and Herald®, 1996.

Stewart, Andrew G. *In Letters of Gold: Heroism for God in the South Seas*. Mountain View, CA: Pacific Press®, 1973.

———. *Trophies From Cannibal Isles*. Washington, DC: Review and Herald®, 1956.

Taylor, R. W. "Alma Wiles—Her Moment of Truth." *South Pacific Record*, March 14, 1987.

Watson, C. H. *Cannibals and Head-hunters: Victories of the Gospel in the South Seas*. Washington, DC: Review and Herald®, 1926.

World Book Encyclopedia. Chicago: World Book/Scott Fetzer, 2016.

Alma Butz as a child with parents Edwin and Florence Butz. The Butz family sailed on the ship *Pitcairn* to Pitcairn Island, where they worked for a year before continuing on to other mission fields in the South Seas.

Norman and Alma Wiles (Adventist Heritage Centre)

The couple met at Avondale College and pioneered the Adventist work among the Big Nambus in the New Hebrides.

Norman and Alma Wiles with three natives. This picture was taken by Martin Johnson, a wildlife photographer from Kansas. The visits of Johnson and his wife, Osa, to Malekula are chronicled in her book *I Married Adventure*.